The Miracle of Self-Love

The Miracle of Self-Love

THE SECRET KEY TO OPEN ALL DOORS

BARBEL MOHR
and MANFRED MOHR

HAY HOUSE
Australia • Canada • Hong Kong • India
South Africa • United Kingdom • United States

First published and distributed in the United Kingdom by:
Hay House UK Ltd, Astley House, 33 Notting Hill Gate, London W11 3JQ.
Tel.: +44 (0)20 3675 2450; Fax: +44 (0)20 3675 2451.
www.hayhouse.co.uk

Published and distributed in the United States of America by:
Hay House, Inc., PO Box 5100, Carlsbad, CA 92018-5100.
Tel.: (1) 760 431 7695 or (800) 654 5126; Fax: (1) 760 431 6948 or (800) 650 5115.
www.hayhouse.com

Published and distributed in Australia by:
Hay House Australia Ltd, 18/36 Ralph St, Alexandria NSW 2015.
Tel.: (61) 2 9669 4299; Fax: (61) 2 9669 4144.
www.hayhouse.com.au

Published and distributed in the Republic of South Africa by:
Hay House SA (Pty), Ltd, PO Box 990, Witkoppen 2068.
Tel./Fax: (27) 11 467 8904. www.hayhouse.co.za

Published and distributed in India by:
Hay House Publishers India, Muskaan Complex, Plot No.3, B-2, Vasant Kunj,
New Delhi – 110 070. Tel.: (91) 11 4176 1620; Fax: (91) 11 4176 1630.
www.hayhouse.co.in

Distributed in Canada by:
Raincoast, 9050 Shaughnessy St, Vancouver, BC V6P 6E5.
Tel.: (1) 604 323 7100; Fax: (1) 604 323 2600

A catalogue record for this book is available from the British Library.

Translation by Andrea Maier and Nick Handforth, www.citylanguages.eu

Interior images © Shutterstock

ISBN: 978-1-78180-054-6

Printed and bound in Great Britain by TJ International, Padstow, Cornwall.

Contents

Preface

As so often is the case with me, this book came about because I had to deal with this problem myself. I know what some of you might be thinking: 'What, her? She must be head over heels in love with herself already…' and wouldn't that be just lovely! Although I am not dealing with this issue for the first time, it always amazes me how well you can hide old thought patterns from yourself deep inside, without even noticing.

Here's an example – and I don't care if anyone laughs at me, I certainly love myself enough to be able to handle that. I tend to wander through life in an unsuspecting, sometimes slightly naive way, and to assume that everybody I meet has good intentions towards me. But this is not always the case. Time and again, people manage to wrap me around their little finger, or to convince me to do something that is good for them, but not for me. I often find the amount of things I am supposed to take care of simply overwhelming. Usually I don't notice at the time, and agree to everything like a good girl, only to regret it two days later.

In these situations, I used to think that it was impossible to go back on a promise. And, at the same time, I beat myself up about the fact that I had been so stupid to agree to do it in the first place. So I tried to train myself to be more careful, so that this kind of thing wouldn't happen to me anymore. When that didn't work at all, I convinced myself that I was just incapable of being more careful, and the same thing kept on happening to me over and over again. Only after my in-depth self-love training did three things change.

First, I realized that I don't want to go through life being careful all the time. I want to stay the way I am, and that's exactly what I do.

Second, I allow myself to cancel things I have previously agreed to, no matter how long it takes me to realize that something about it isn't right for me. So the other person gave it a try, and it looked like they would get their way. Well, bad luck! I will cancel whenever it feels right for me, and if someone gets annoyed then that's their problem.

Third, I speak to myself more lovingly. I don't tell myself that I am stupid or incapable anymore. I am allowed to be like this – and I love myself in spite of it.

And, because we are constantly confronted in life with the subject of loving ourselves, Manfred and I have included lots of exercises in this book. You don't have to do all of them, and you are not doing anything wrong if you miss one out. Quite the opposite. The first exercise in loving yourself is to feel what touches your heart and fills it with joy. Start with that precise exercise. Do as many of the exercises as you want and no more. It could be that one exercise alone is enough to change everything, if you do it with ardour and all your heart. Find the ones that suit you. After all, not every exercise can be a hit with everybody.

But whether an exercise has a large or small effect on you, or none at all, is not just about finding the right exercise to suit you. Each exercise can be the right one for you, if you do it gladly and with love.

If you just rush through an exercise in a routine way, it will do you no good at all. But an exercise you do gladly, with love and care, can change everything at a stroke.

Some people even make themselves feel stressed when learning to love themselves: 'Oh no! I only felt happiness while doing the exercise. It is never going to work now, because I forgot to feel care and love'. Forget it! There was nothing missing. First of all, any one of the three qualities is enough. Second, it is completely normal if, at the beginning, you don't feel much or anything at all. If all of us were professionals at loving ourselves, then we wouldn't need this book at all. When children learn to walk, they are very wobbly on their feet, too. But a child still makes progress and gets better day by day. So don't worry, you can be wobbly when you do your love yourself exercises. The more you practise, the easier they will become and the more intensely you will experience how your self-love is increasing.

Have fun!

Barbel and Manfred

P.S. We always address our readers and seminar participants directly as 'you', because we believe we are all travelling along the same road, and so none of us are strangers. We will continue to do so in this book. When 'I' appears in this book, it means that I, Barbel, am writing. Manfred has avoided giving examples using 'I', or chosen to use 'we'.

'All the love of this world
is based on self-love.'

Meister Eckhart

Part 1

Not Every First Step is Difficult

Is Loving Yourself Really Okay?

♥♥♥♥

'But is it actually okay to love yourself? Isn't that just so self-satisfying and aggrandizing, mindlessly vain, egotistical and simply outrageous?' This is the gist of the question that a married Indian couple once asked me during a lecture in London. And there is a very simple answer to it: loving yourself is so important because you can only give to others what you already have. If you have no love, you won't have anything to pass on either. This is why we need to love ourselves. If no one were able to pass on love unless they had previously received love, then love would have long since died out, because we would all just be waiting for someone else to start. Love only works when each one of us finds the source for love within ourselves – completely independent from the outside world. This means, then, that loving yourself is not only okay, it is also the prerequisite that allows us to love others, to be charitable and benevolent.

I'm happy to share my views on loving yourself with you in this book, but I have to ask you to do one thing: no matter what I say or write, check in your heart, to see what is right and makes sense for you. The only real way for anyone to grow and develop is if each of us learns how to examine our heart to find our own truth – and not simply to parrot what somebody else says, no matter how good it might sound at the time.

The ability to check something against your heart is an integral part of loving yourself. Someone who does not love themself, or sees themself as being worth less than others, will tend to believe that other people's views are more important than their own, and will be too timid to follow the truth of their heart. They will not listen at all (or not listen properly) to the impulses, hints and inspiration that flow from within them. 'It's not that important; it's just my silly subconscious talking, my petty little childish impulses. Who am I to know, anyway…?'

They will not trust themself to say 'no' when all of those around them are saying 'yes, yes, yes!' – even when it's all too obvious that they aren't speaking from the heart. For us to be self-reliant and imbue our actions with the greatest amount of truth, purity and love possible, it is important to act towards ourselves in a loving and trusting manner. We can learn again how to recognize and follow the wisdom of our heart, our intuition and gut feelings.

'Your task is not to seek for love, but merely to seek and find all the barriers within yourself that you have built against it.'

Rumi

This is why it is so vital, first of all, to find out what you really like, what is important to you and what you want to spend your time doing.

Exercise

Make a list of 30 things that you like doing. This can be anything: having good conversations, going for walks, reading, listening to music, dancing, meeting friends, baking cakes…

- Then ask yourself when was the last time you did each of these things. What have you been doing instead?
- Also ask yourself how you really want to live: how many web contacts and how many personal contacts do you want to maintain?
- How much time do you really want to spend on emails, the internet, your mobile phone, or watching TV? How many of them actually make you happy? What are you missing out on that might be more important to you?

Is there already anything that you want to change in your life, and can change, when you look at this list?

Tip

If your list looks like this:

- *Shopping*
- *High society parties*
- *Drinking*
- *Shopping*
- *Shopping*
- *Shopping*
- *Helicopter rides*
- *Skiing*
- *Going on cruises*
- *Trips around the world*

...then I have some special advice for you: try spending 30 days in the desert doing survival training. This will probably awaken completely new interests in you.

♥ ♥ ♥ ♥

Three years ago, we had a boy au pair staying with us, whose parents had sent him off to a kind of survival camp in the woods as a punishment for getting bad grades at school.

The only food the children had was what they were able to find in the woods. Life there was devoid of any comfort or luxury. At first he was just horrified, but after a while a love for nature and simplicity and joy in communal living awoke within him. When he returned home, his parents were waiting for him and feeling guilty that their punishment might have been a bit harsh. They were then completely amazed to see their boy return full of enthusiasm, wanting to sign up straight away for the next camp. He had turned around 180 degrees over those three weeks.

♡♡♡

The Miracle of Loving Yourself

The miracle of loving yourself begins to take effect right here. We have often simply adapted our lifestyle to the conventions of our environment. We don't even ask ourselves the question: 'What do I actually want?' Just being aware of this fact can cause true miracles to occur. Suddenly, you know what you have to do to feel more satisfied and fulfilled again. Most of the items on the list are usually very simple things that cost only a little money to do, or nothing at all. It feels wonderful just to be doing more of these things again.

No-ageing and the Decline of Self-love

An important aspect of loving yourself is demonstrated by how we cope with the way we look. There is a real fashion for model shows on TV and after watching them, many women feel even older and more ugly than before. Could it be that the association for cosmetic surgeons sponsor these shows? According to the German magazine *Focus* we will have to get used to the fact that we'll become social pariahs if we don't get injections to remove wrinkles, or cosmetic surgery and the like in the future. 'Anti-ageing' is out, 'no-ageing' and 'down-ageing' have become the new trends that lead to social acceptability. Brrrr, it sends a shiver down my spine when I put it so succinctly, and I will tell you what I think of doing about it: I will dye my hair grey now – yup, right now (it is half grey already). And I will found a new society: 'Old and ugly? Then come and join us! Free membership and an old fogey badge for over 35s'.

Would someone who loved themself choose to have cosmetic surgery? Certainly far less often than someone who is tormented by self-doubt and always judges themself harshly. At the moment, I would not choose to go under the knife for the sake of beauty, for one thing because I am too vain. Yes, that's right, too vain. I simply don't want to look as ugly as people do, up close, after multiple cosmetic surgery operations. Not even if it might make me look really great from a distance in heavily overexposed photographs.

Over 20 years ago, I worked for a short time as a photo assistant in show business, and met one of Michael Jackson's sisters at a photo shoot. She was still young at the time but even then you couldn't help but feel terrified if you got closer than five metres to her. In spite of the centimetre-thick make-up, you could see the scars shining through in many places on her face. That kind of thing scares me. I would get nightmares from Dr Frankenstein and Co. if I had to see my reflection in the mirror looking like that.

So vanity is one of the reasons why I would prefer to save myself from that fate. The scars become more evident the older you get, and some make it necessary to have even more operations. But anyway, let's spare ourselves the details. The other reason I don't want to have cosmetic surgery is the fear that I would no longer be recognized – that my spirit would no longer be recognizable, is what I mean. I believe that nature gives us a specific form, that our physiognomy is an expression of our soul, and that our personality and character are reflected in our facial expression. If I want to find and attract people who suit me, the way I truly am, then I must also actually look like me.

Squirrel or swan?

To put it into pictures: if a squirrel had an operation to make it look like a swan, because that's what is 'in' at the moment, then, on the one hand, it will attract real swans on the lookout for other members of their species, and on the other, all the other creatures looking to be in contact with a swan. All of the squirrels, though, will avoid him. Being a squirrel, I am only able to feel fully comfortable and at ease with other squirrels. So I would be pretty daft to have an operation to become a swan, or even to dress myself up as one. And anyway, there is no reason why I can't be friends with swans as a squirrel, and certainly not by just having my neck elongated through an operation. There is a very different way to do this: swans, just like all other extremely beautiful, normal and ugly creatures, feel attracted to squirrels that radiate self-love, warmth and contented self-awareness.

Who wants perfection anyway?

Back to us humans. The process of turning 'from human to zombie' through too much cosmetic surgery and Botox is familiar to almost everyone – at least from photos. The examples we know look so unnatural and ghoulish that you automatically flinch when you see one face to face. Instead of becoming accepted and admired by more people, they are most likely to scare them away. And this is even with the techniques of photo processing available today, which can be used to cheat and make a person look great in photos without the need for any operation or facial scarring. When my stepfather sees my publicity photos, he always asks me who is the 15-year-younger girl I persuaded to double for me. There is a 'photo gallery' on my home page (www.baerbelmohr.de) under 'CV'. I thought it was dishonest only to use publicity shots, so I have posted a few more realistic photos there, and I really enjoy looking at these honest (sometimes maybe even too honest) images of myself. They are much more entertaining than just the sterile publicity photos. And anyway, perfection just breeds aggression because it gives many people the feeling that they can't compete, have too many faults and that they are, therefore, worth less. The seemingly perfect person radiates the message, 'look how wonderful I am, and how terrible you are!' This repels other people and makes them feel aggressive. Yet it is precisely the small faults and human weaknesses that make us loveable. The slanted and skewed is usually much funnier and livelier.

But I still want to stress that I do not condemn anyone who chooses to have cosmetic surgery. It depends on the situation and the extent. Besides, all people, whether lifted or not, can still turn their self-doubt into self-confidence. And if you find warmth and unconditional self-love radiating from a surgically wrinkle-free face, you'll quickly forget everything else. The following exercise has already helped many people to accept and love themselves more and more.

Exercise

I first recommended this exercise (in a slightly different form) in a book I wrote at the end of the last millennium. I was shown it by an American therapist. In the meantime, lots of people have got to know about it through many different sources. It's the love yourself mirror exercise – a real classic for dealing with problems with loving yourself or the way you look.

Stand in front of a full-length mirror, or the largest mirror you have, and love yourself just the way you are. As, admittedly, this is not quite as easily done as said, you can also start in a very small way and work yourself up. Find a part of your body that you like, any part at all!

A typical exercise could start like this:

- Day 1: 'So, you ugly toad, I am supposed to love you, how in heaven's name am I going to manage that?'
- Day 2: 'I like my firm calves. They would even appeal to David Beckham. Okay, you toady calves, I'm blowing you a kiss.'

- Day 3: 'Actually, my ears aren't that bad either, at least they don't stick out…'
- Day 4: 'My third molar from the back on the left still looks pretty good. Can you hear me, boy? I love you! Kiss, kiss.'
- Day 5: 'Wow, now I actually love three things about myself: my calves, ears and one tooth. And, if I look at them properly, my arms look pretty normal, too. There are certainly uglier arms about. Dear arms, I love you both.'
- Day 6: 'My big toe looks cool! Hey mate, I like you.'
- Day 7: 'Hmm, I think my tummy is feeling left out. I can really tell it is feeling upset. Well, here it goes… Dear wobbly tummy, I love you too – a little bit. You shouldn't feel sad…'

And all you have to do is carry on like this. You'll see your body just loves it. Keep going, and increase your love bit by bit. One fine day you will be able to thank every part of your body for enabling you to experience life as a human being. Love each part of your body, just the way it is. Supposedly ugly people need just as much love as everyone else, and the same goes for supposedly ugly parts of your body, which also need just as much love as all of the others.

No matter whether you are practising with a single part or your entire body, this exercise strengthens your immune system, your intuition and your self-love – all at the same time. Take the time to examine each part of your body properly and send it love and warmth from the bottom of your heart.

You can't do this exercise too often. You can also greet yourself with love every morning before you brush your teeth, once you've had a bit of practice in liking yourself. Gaze deeply into your eyes and look for your inner beauty. The more often you look for it, the more happily it will surface from the depths of your soul.

The Miracle of Loving Yourself

Whatever you do, love yourself for doing it, love your individuality and your own particular style. Even if you have 20 cosmetic surgery operations behind you already, it is never too late to add inner beauty, too! And for the rest of us, it's very clear that strengthening our inner beauty and self-love is, first, cheaper than having an operation and, second, raises our power to attract other friendly, warm people – in a wonderful way, far more than any operation ever could.

Better Relationships Thanks to Loving Yourself

♥♥♥♥

Loving yourself is the foundation for a happy life – and not only because of your inner happiness. Your external happiness is also heavily dependent on it. For a long time, the idea that a person emits vibrations was dismissed as esoteric frippery. Then neuroscientists such as Joachim Bauer discovered mirror neurons. These prove that we can feel the emotions of those around us. If, for example, the centre for emotional pain is activated within me, it activates the mirror neurons of every person I come into contact with. Something within the other person detects how I feel and whether I love myself or not. And then it doesn't matter whether I am looking for new friends, a new partner, a new job, or trying to make a good impression on a potential landlord. The more self-love I send out, the better my chances will be. A person who loves themself radiates much more clearly who they actually are. The effect is more authentic and attracts people who really suit them. Of course, it is possible that it will beam a few people away, who come from a completely different emotional star. But seen in the long run, this is far more of a blessing than a curse.

Just imagine that you are trying to find your dream apartment: beautiful, bright, quiet, with a garden and affordable. You find it, but 100 other people come to the viewing as well. Each one of them wants the apartment. What now? The landlord is undecided. Who should he pick from such a choice? He welcomes each one with a handshake and most of the prospective tenants probably send out the message: 'Oh well, it would be fantastic, but I can already see that my chances are low…' Then you come along (having worked your way through this book) and send out a very different message: 'What a wonderful apartment, this is exactly what I'd imagined. And because I love myself, I trust that life will love me, too. If I don't get this apartment, then I am sure to find one just as beautiful, or maybe even better, somewhere else. I am sure that life is on my side…' (This is the typical approach of people with a healthy level of self-love.) You are cheerful and open for anything. The landlord shakes your hand and gives an involuntary sigh of relief – finally, someone radiating a relaxed attitude. And hey presto – you get the apartment. Unless, of course, there is someone else who has a stronger resonance with the landlord, who somehow feels even more suitable or maybe more familiar to him. But that can only mean that there is another apartment waiting for you, where you'll be even more welcome in the neighbourhood, and where everything else will suit you much better as well.

Vibrations count

Landlords and bosses make choices – usually without consciously noticing – according to their emotions and first impressions. 'Which person gives me the feeling that matches my expectations? Who do I feel attracted to?' And: 'What vibration is that person sending out?' This last point plays a decisive role, and you can influence it. If you feel relaxed with yourself, then others will equally feel relaxed with you. Love yourself and others will find it easier to love you.

If you are often invited to job interviews but never get the job, you could take a little break from applying and first work on loving yourself. Let's put it to the test. Just imagine that you are the boss of a company and you interview two applicants. Applicant A has the necessary qualifications, but radiates uncertainty and a large amount of self-doubt. How do you feel about the prospect of hiring her? Applicant B also has the necessary qualifications, but radiates optimism and a healthy level of self-love. How do you feel about the prospect of hiring her? When it comes down to it, it is this exact feeling the other person generates within us, which is decisive in accepting or rejecting the applicant.

It is, perhaps, most obvious in romantic relationships. If I radiate the fact that I am not worth loving, then I will find it hard to find someone who loves me. If I radiate that I am amazingly loveable, lots of people will feel attracted to me. So the period in which you are single is the perfect time for you to improve your love for yourself. You will only be able to find someone to be in a loving relationship with you if you are truly in touch with your own heart, if you open your heart first to yourself, and then to others. In addition, every relationship will improve if people in it love themselves. A person who loves themself is more ready to take on responsibility for themself, and not blame their partner for things that they often can't do anything about. The lower your level of self-love, the more you are likely to view each free expression of your partner's personality as offensive. This reminds me of a joke. She writes in her diary: 'Dear diary, it's all over, I am totally depressed, I am certain he doesn't love me anymore. He hasn't spoken a word to me since last night; he just looks right through me. I know he has met someone else, it's all over, boohoohoo…' He writes in his diary: 'It's all over. My football team has lost…'

This is a common occurrence. Someone who does not love themself is certain from the outset that everyone is against them. A person who loves themself is certain that they are worth loving. They are less likely to believe that the frustration the other person is feeling has anything to do with them. And, anyway, you have nothing to lose if you

'If you love yourself,
you love everybody else
as you do yourself.'

Meister Eckhart

love yourself. So you simply ask, 'Darling, what's up? You look so down.' A person who loves themself will ask this question in an interested, open and loving tone of voice and is most likely to get a proper answer. Someone who does not love themself will automatically tend to ask this same question with an affronted, mistrustful underlying tone and will receive a snotty answer from their partner, who is feeling depressed already. And the typical result? 'I knew it! He doesn't love me anymore!'

Exercise

Observe yourself and the people around you. How do you get on with the people you come into contact with in your daily life? How much do you think they love themselves? How do you feel when you are with each one of them? Can you tell the difference between real, relaxed, natural self-confidence and assumed arrogance? How do you react emotionally to others? How do they react to you? Can you tell from the reactions of others how much self-confidence or self-doubt you are currently radiating? Treat the exercise as a game that will help you learn more about yourself and come a little closer to yourself. Because true love – even self-love – requires closeness.

- Imagine a person who loves themself and thanks creation for their own wonderful existence. This person, filled with inner love, meets you, looks into your eyes and immediately thinks you are nice. You get to know each other and you really feel completely loved and accepted by them. How does that feel? What kind of images form inside you about such a friendship or relationship? What course could it take?

- Now imagine another person. This person does not love themself. This person believes self-love is equal to vanity and forbids themself from having it. They do not want to give their own opinion too much weight, because other people usually know better. This person lacks love, and desperately needs some. Now they meet you. They look into your eyes and a spark of hope ignites within them. 'This might be a person I could love, if they first give me the love I have been yearning for and have needed for such a long time…' You get to know each other better and this person swears to love you forever, and tells you how much they need you. How does that feel? What kind of images form inside you about this kind of friendship or relationship? What course could it take? Which kind of affection or love feels better to you? Which feels more genuine? What do you feel inside you when you picture these two people? Sure, the second person will probably be deeply

> faithful to you. They are much too insecure ever to leave you. But do you feel properly loved because of it, or more like you are being used as their personal reservoir of energy? Can you really be yourself beside a person with such a deficit of love? Or does this person cry out in panic every time you want to do something for yourself, without them? Do you have to be available to calm their fears, or are you really allowed to live out your true life with this person at your side?

With these questions I only want to draw your attention to this point. There are no universally true answers, just a myriad of possible combinations, such as the following two. If someone, say, has an 80 per cent level of love for themself already and just still 'needs' you a little bit in order not to feel worthless, then maybe this is exactly the right amount for you to get a feeling of security. If, on the other hand, someone is hovering around at a level of 10 per cent love for themself, a person with a level of 50 per cent might already intimidate them.

The Miracle of Loving Yourself

If you do not love yourself much and you strain to wring affection from others, you can wrestle for a long time and still achieve very little. If, on the other hand, you develop more love for yourself, then a miracle will happen. Others will approach you of their own accord and seek out your company.

I Did That Really Well!

♥♥♥♥

Our little daughter hates maths, although it was always my favourite subject when I was at school. She recently came home feeling very sad. They had gone through the times tables at school, and she hadn't understood a word. She didn't even understand what this 'times' thing was supposed to mean.

Mummy can explain, don't worry: 'If you buy one times five soft toys at school, how many soft toys do you have? Five. If we then go back to the zoo the next day and you buy five more soft toys, then you have bought two times five, so how many do you have then? Ten, of course!' Our daughter loves soft toys. She never loses track of them. She can work out anything in soft toys, or scoops of ice cream. Eating six scoops of ice cream on four consecutive days, that's 6+6+6+6, and makes 24, that is obvious. So she has finally also understood that multiplication is a kind of reduced addition. So far, so good. But when I said: 'See, you have understood it', she bristled and said: 'No, I still don't understand any of it!' And she really didn't understand it when we did the next exercise.

***MB** (Mummy Barbel):* 'Look, you were able to do everything here. Tell yourself: I did that really well!' But oh no, that was impossible. My daughter disappeared under the table, her head under the chair with her legs in the air. She hid like an ostrich, stuck her head in the sand and was gone.

MB: 'Why don't you want to say it?'

Child: 'I haaaaaaaaate maths!'

MB: 'I understand. But do you know, your gut feeling and your subconscious are always listening to what you say. If you say that you don't understand it, although you have just done it really well, then your subconscious thinks that you want to forget it all again straight away – and then you'll have to do maths much more often, until you understand it. If, on the other hand, you say to yourself very often, "I did that really well!", then your subconscious will think: "Aha! If that is the case, I will remember it." And then you'll only have to do maths half as often.'

Child: 'But I haaaaaaaaate maths.'

MB: 'Do you want to do less maths?'

Child: 'Yes!'

MB: 'Then you should praise yourself whenever you get something right and you'll be free of your maths exercises much more quickly. Just give it a go, say: "I did that really well…"'

The child huffs, whines and complains, but finally – still upside down with her head under the chair – she giggles and a 'I did that really well' comes out. I decided not to bother her with maths for the rest of the day. At lunch she asked: 'Mummy, do you think I still know what 5x5 equals?'

'I bet you don't.'

She trumpeted '25' and went through all of the exercises we had done with soft toys and scoops of ice cream again in her head. She could still do all of them. And this time it was easier for her to say: 'I really did that well!' She was suddenly so happy and relieved that she'd understood how stupid multiplication worked, that after lunch she sat down and wrote down the entire multiplication table again and worked it all out by herself. All of a sudden, she could do it. 'I really did that very well!' She was so happy.

Later, I thought about why she had vehemently refused at first to say 'I really did that well!'. The sentence did not seem to fit with her disgust for maths at all. It was as if she'd be switching to join the maths-lovers' camp, if she admitted to having worked something out well. But she didn't want to become a maths fan, like her brother, mother and father. Because maths fans do a lot of maths. But she wanted to be rid of her exercises as quickly as possible. This mechanism often appears with adults as well; we don't enjoy something, so we have to reject it and be against it, in order to be rid of it more quickly. But the exact opposite is actually true: rejection acts like glue.

Exercise

Praise yourself when you do anything you don't like doing or are not good at, for every little success. You'll see that you will finish the task you dislike ever faster. And bit by bit your image of yourself will also change because of it. Instead of 'I am just much too stupid to do this or that', your subconscious will suddenly think: 'I can manage this or that. I use my own method and always find a way to tackle it. I am simply just a wonderful person'. This is the real trick. If you praise yourself for even small successes, your feeling of self-confidence rises and you increasingly trust yourself to do more in all areas of your life.

You can multiply this effect by praising yourself for everything that works out well for you and that you have done well. Not in a vain way: 'Nana-nanana, I am the best', but in a thankful way: 'I am glad of my strengths and abilities and thankful for them.'

Tip

It is sometimes fun to compare yourself to others, and it can spur you on to do even better. But sometimes comparing yourself can just be frustrating. It is usually counterproductive to compare yourself to other people for tasks that you have to do anyway, but find difficult. It is better to compare what you used to be able to do, with what you are able to do now. Look at your own progress and rejoice in it. And if you are the best in any particular thing you do, be glad of your ability and help others not to become frustrated because they are not as good as you. This will also help you to develop the habit of being loving towards yourself when something doesn't work out straight away.

The Miracle of Loving Yourself

Just a moment ago I understood nothing – but with a bit of self-praise it's like clockwork. Even difficult things can become wonderfully easy through self-reinforcement, and you will often do it differently than others, and find your own individual method. A further reason to be proud of yourself. Award yourself the 'Nobel Prize for positive self-motivation'.

Simply Reverse Your Obstructive Beliefs

♥♥♥♥

If we are not careful, our daughter will convince herself by saying, 'I will never understand maths' and be tortured by it through all her years at school. Although, with a bit of help, we have seen that it takes very little to change a child's belief from 'I never understand maths' into 'I can understand everything'.

Such childhood beliefs are often the reason why, as adults, we don't trust ourselves to do something, or allow ourselves to fully and completely love ourselves, just the way we are. Although most people can do some things better and other things worse than most other people. Anyone who has read books such as *Rich Dad, Poor Dad: What the Rich Teach Their Kids About Money* by Robert T. Kiyosaki or just observes real life knows that good grades in school are far from being the only road to success. But so many young people still carry many complexes from childhood into adult life. This is completely unnecessary and a crying shame.

Sometimes it is common sense 'truths' such as 'no pain, no gain', which we still hear echoing in our ears from when we were young and which make us believe that we have to fight to achieve every little thing. 'After all, there is no such thing as a free lunch', we think and are not surprised. In truth, however, this saying is just an unhelpful doctrine from our childhood. Of course, it is true that not much will happen if you just lie around in your hammock doing nothing. But whether what you do bears fruit often, or seldom, greatly depends on your subconscious imprints.

There is, however, a really clever piece of wisdom, which in essence says 'Successful people are not more successful than others because they've had fewer failures, but because they've tried more often'. Although my experience of life is that with a bit of 'cosmic guidance' and good intuition, you can certainly reduce the number of failures significantly, the difference between successful and unsuccessful people still remains, that the former believe in themselves, no matter what happens, and the others give up after just a few flops.

Recognizing your imprints

Behind these failures lie unhelpful beliefs about ourselves. So let's get rid of them and replace them with new, helpful imprints. This can also happen quite easily, as with Dieter from the 'Positive Factory' who I have worked with many times. He really is one in a million and a bundle of energy who has been successfully working for many years as a personality trainer. Having a child with so much energy apparently overwhelmed his mother. When, for example, he came downstairs in the morning whistling and singing, it was simply too much for her: 'Birds that sing in the morning get screwed by the cat when evening comes', she would say in annoyance.

And Dieter, the shocked little bird, shut his beak. But the bird grew bigger and wanted to sing again. Somewhere along the road to finding himself, he remembered these unhelpful imprints. And then he had an ingenious idea. All he did was alter the saying a little bit, so that it sounded almost exactly the same, but had the opposite meaning. The wonderful thing about this reframing is that your subconscious believes that it has just been making a mistake all of these years, and completely misunderstood the message. And abracadabra – it changes everything around and you can sing happily once again, be free to believe in yourself again and all of the rest.

How did Dieter change the saying? He gave it a new, very personal flavour: 'Birds that sing in the morning screw the cat when evening comes'. Since changing his doctrine, Dieter now sings with special joy in the mornings.

However you choose to reverse your negative beliefs, the most important thing is always to change your beliefs in a way that feels right and good for you, and that you enjoy them. They don't need to please anybody except you.

Exercise

Make a list of obstructive beliefs that have influenced you. If you can't think of any right away, you can always start by going over common sayings and listening in to yourself to find out if any of them blocks you. Another way would be to Google 'proverbs' or 'clichés' and see which of them give you a bad, or good, feeling. Once you've established one or more beliefs, you can go ahead and look for a suitable way to reverse them. Here are a few examples:

- 'You can't teach an old dog new tricks.' That could also go like this: 'You can teach an old dog tricks a puppy couldn't do.' Or 'Old dog or young dog, everyone loves to learn!'
- 'No pain, no gain.' This way sounds much more convincing to me 'No pain, much gain'. Yeah!
- 'There's no such thing as a free lunch.' Why not change it to 'Giving and being given to are great – remember life itself was given to me too!'
- 'Business before pleasure.' How about this one 'All my business is pure pleasure' or 'The right kind of business is also pleasure'.

Create little affirmation cards with your new beliefs and repeat them every morning and evening three times each. What's important here is to feel the meaning of your reversed belief. Simply rattling it off won't do the trick, try to actually feel the meaning as intensively as you can. Visualize yourself and how you approach life with this new belief.

Even well-intended wisdoms may backfire: 'The eagle flies alone, geese in flocks.' Some will like hearing that, as it justifies their loner way of life. Others might feel encouraged to think that it'd be a good idea to become a lonely eagle, even if they were actually a sociable goose. Or 'All things come to those who wait.' That might well be the case, but if you are a start-up type of person this sentence could ruin your spontaneity. And how about 'Variety is the spice of life.' If you like having a spicy bit on the side every now and then, you will feel encouraged to keep it up. If you are, however, a faithful, committed person, this sentence could handicap your relationship.

Nothing applies to everyone. Work out what blocks you, and what is good for you. A sentence that is just right for one person to affirm their belief, will mean total self-denial for another person. Focus on the beliefs slumbering inside you and pin down the ones that are obstructive. Maybe this exercise will bring back some very individual childhood beliefs you kept being told, such as 'If you behave like that, I won't love you anymore or 'Lazy, silly child, why are you always doing this and that…' or 'Stop showing off all the time. A child should remain modest and humble'. And then, you take those sentences and twist them around!

The Miracle of Loving Yourself

You don't need to find the central theme to your life right away to give some positive changes a nudge. Taking a step-by-step approach towards yourself and self-confidence will do just fine. Sometimes, a single intense experience with a new belief is enough to make you appear and act like a brand new person. All of a sudden, you are able to do what seemed impossible, or a fear that has always stood in your way disappears… Reversing obstructive beliefs can turn you into your own private 'miracle healer'.

The Strength Behind Weakness

♥♥♥♥

For my birthday I often receive a range of beautiful greeting cards containing wise sayings. Something along the lines: 'Only the body ages. The spirit essentially remains the same, as it was when we were 20. With a bit of luck, we might have become somewhat wiser, but never wise enough to understand why the body just doesn't stay as young as we feel.' So true. Last time (my 46th birthday) someone sent me a particularly pertinent story – unfortunately, it didn't mention the author – which fits well here:

> 'Every day, an old woman took two big bowls to a source of water. She had attached the two vessels to the ends of a long pole, which she carried over her shoulders. One of the water bowls, however, had a crack halfway through it, so that she always lost half the water on the way back home. This went

on for two years, and the cracked bowl felt terribly ashamed. It finally told the old woman that it felt awful because of its shameful inability to perform.

The old woman, however, smiled kindly (perfectly appropriate behaviour, of course, in a proper wisdom story) and said: "My dear water bowl, have you never noticed that on your side of the path flowers are blooming? Being well aware of your flaw, I planted flowers along this side. You have been watering them every day with the water dripping from your leak. For two years, I have been able to pick fresh flowers every day to adorn our table. Without you, this beauty would not exist. You are unique, beautiful, and precious – precisely because you are the way you are." ***

The bowl thanked the old woman for her wise and loving words and stuck out its tongue at the undamaged bowl: "Pah, you boring, perfect thing, I'm the best!"

But the old woman spoke out: "My dear water bowl, please don't turn into a self-indulging narcissist to compensate for the complexes you had before, that doesn't suit you either. Everyone is beautiful and precious in his or her own way. After all, the other bowl brings home more water, which I also appreciate very much."

At that, the water bowl felt ashamed once more, saying, "You are right, I'm sorry.'"

And here is the moral of the story: you should not pride yourself too much on your flaws and weaknesses, after you have understood that they are not flaws, but precious characteristics. Everyone should make the best out of their own nature.

All right, I have to admit, the original story is a tiny bit shorter, and I added the moral.

Exercise

Read the story again up to the *** and think about whether your flaws and weaknesses have advantages too, or have brought about positive results and developments, which would not have taken place had you been flawless and perfect. So, now get going on your exercise, please. It really is worthwhile and will open your eyes!

Okay then, let's assume you have done the exercise. Now I'll give you another example of how a few flaws can enrich your life. One of my publishers has just been around to visit. He is convinced that he has no feeling for language whatsoever. Makes you wonder how he managed to become a publisher, doesn't it? He simply sees and feels the energy in books. If he feels touched by a book and likes its energy, he publishes it. If he doesn't, he won't. Perfection is boring if it fails to touch you, and pretty words alone don't make a book worth reading. That's how he sees it, anyway. If his feeling for language were more refined, his other power of perception might never have developed in this way.

Special gifts

The lack of a certain skill or characteristic often creates room for something else to unfold, something special and unique, something wonderful. In one way or the other, there is a strength hidden behind each and every weakness. Either another skill balances out the weakness, as we have seen in the examples of the water bowl and the publisher's lack of feeling for language. Or a person is, in fact, more than capable of doing exactly the one thing they think they can't – provided they allow themself to develop their own style.

By way of example, leaving school and not writing a word for ten years left me with a fairly rough-and-ready writing style. Any knowledge of spelling and punctuation I ever had deserted me. I would never have thought I could become an author, let alone a successful one. What gave me comfort was when the chief editor of a major women's magazine once emailed me an unedited interview article before publishing. I loved it, because I saw she had made at least as many mistakes as I did. This showed me that I'm not the only one who makes a living out of writing without a polished style or perfect spelling. It's not that I actively refuse to write correctly, I just keep forgetting the rules. That is one of my weaknesses. And yet, at the same time, writing is one of my strengths.

There are also many successful speakers who, when they were younger, were unable to say peep if more than three people were around. When I gave my first lecture in front of 14 people, it took a full bottle of valerian juice to calm me down. Back then I never would have thought that one day I would actually enjoy public speaking.

Exercise

Make a list of your flaws and weaknesses. Consider the possibility that there might be hidden strengths behind them. Is there anything that comes to mind? What kind of strength could emerge from it? Start by writing down the opposite of each flaw and weakness you have listed. In doing so, you may just stumble upon one of your potential skills that have been in hiding inside you. Acknowledging them is the first step in reawakening them with a kiss. The second step will take self-confidence and the ability to love yourself, for you to actually dare to develop the particular strength. Your path will always be different to everyone else's and there is no ready-made recipe.

Let me give you a few examples. A cold personality might conceal a warm, emotional heart. Slow thinking may just be confused with careful consideration. Weak rhetorical skills could hide strong heart-to-heart communication skills. Impatience might obscure real patience. The inability to handle criticism could hide the ability to express constructive criticism and to discover new ways of social interaction. Aggression might conceal a gentle heart. Behind fear, there might be trust.

The Miracle of Loving Yourself

Loving yourself can help you start listening to your heart, not your head. It can give you the courage to permanently shift your perception by 30 centimetres, from your head to your heart, and to turn a weakness (the inability to listen to your heart) into a strength (always/mostly listening to your heart). The miracle of loving yourself can help an anxious person become courageous. Loving yourself can free you from paying too much attention to other people's opinions – and make you feel more courageous on the way. Loving yourself can create a link between your intuition and your feelings. The ability to love yourself is the crucial factor for turning your weakness into strength.

Saying 'No' for Love's Sake

I was born under the sign of Cancer and fit the cliché that the Cancerian character has an often overly pronounced need for harmony. In the past, I quite often said 'yes' just for the sake of peace and harmony. However, this can be something of a shortcoming if you have an international career (one that pretty much caught me off guard by arriving out of the blue), which involves requests from a range of countries, countless promoters, private individuals, companies, publishers, people interested in working together and so on and so forth. Of course, all this is really nice and a big blessing – please keep putting forward your requests, everybody. I had to learn, however, to say 'no' without feeling guilty.

For a while I had to turn down 90 per cent of all requests out of simple lack of time (things have fortunately calmed down a bit in the meantime). Not everyone was able to understand that, though: 'Uhuh, now she's getting pretentious, guess she's too good for that now…', or, 'She's got a nerve, don't her readers pay her income, how can she dare to make herself unavailable…' and so on. And what did the harmony-seeking part of me do? It strived to evade the reproaches and accusations and to please as many people as it could. So I took on more commitments than I could handle. Bit by bit the tension grew, and I was increasingly unable to deal with the pressure, and increasingly agreed to do more and more things which my heart was telling me not to.

The result was that after a few years I was so exhausted that I went through a massive burnout period and needed a year-long break to recover (having such a wonderful job, this is quite embarrassing, really). And for whose benefit? Certainly not mine, nor my health's or family's – and neither for the benefit of my readers and seminar participants! First of all, as they were subjected to an extensive, forced break, and second of all, as both the energy I transfer and the energy field that builds up during my work grow much stronger if I am in full power, joy, and love – and certainly not when I feel worn out.

The victim's 'Yes'

There is, however, another reason, why from my point of view today, I consider it unhealthy to say 'yes' when

‘The oldest, shortest words –“yes” and “no” – are those which require the most thought.’

PYTHAGORAS

actually meaning and feeling 'no'. We are all spiritual, divine creatures (I assume that we all agree on this, as otherwise you wouldn't be reading one of my books) and we sense each other's meaning, even if we choose not to express it in words. So I say 'yes' to avoid my counterpart's anger if I had said 'no', or to do the other person a favour, even if this doesn't actually suit me at the moment. What happens? On a deep, spiritual level, the other person can sense that this is no joyful, genuine 'yes'. This, in turn, has an effect on my counterpart. Subconsciously, I'm sending out this message: 'I cannot stay true to myself; you are responsible for the way I feel and for me to take the right decisions. I can't do it by myself. I am afraid of you, and put your needs before my own'.

What's worse is that, from an energetic point of view, we turn the other person into the offender and ourselves into a victim. Is that an expression of love? Absolutely not! What's much more loving is a sympathetic 'no'. A 'no' that results in me enduring the other person's anger or irritation, thinking to myself: 'I understand your disappointment, I see your anger. But I will not turn you into the culprit and myself into the victim. Even if you feel upset with me, I remain surrounded by love and I stand up for my own truth. This way I feel better, and you stay free from the energetic guilt I would bring upon you if I let you turn me into the victim that allows you to put pressure on me.'

Exercise

Start by listening in to yourself – whether your 'yes' or 'no' really comes from the heart in harmless situations. Let me give you an example: Someone would like to borrow a book from you. If you truly want to lend it, say 'yes!' If, however, you already know this would be the last time you will see it and you'll have to buy a new one? If you don't want that to happen, say 'no'. But maybe you also think that you are not going to touch the book again anyway, and that it would therefore be okay if you never get it back. Think about your answer and only say 'yes' if you can happily give it to him or her with your heart.

We often avoid saying 'no' out of fear of putting off or hurting someone. Most of the time though, the other person will understand if we express ourselves with love. Therefore, make yourself a list of tenderly expressed 'no' statements, so that you won't ever have to fear saying 'no' again. Let's just take the example above with the book that you'd rather not lend out. Instead of saying, 'No, you're never going to give it back anyway!' which is not very diplomatic and likely to cause offence, you could say, 'I am very attached to this book, I'd rather not lend it out.'

Go over at least another five to ten examples and think of friendly, soft variations for saying 'no'.

♡♡♡

The Miracle of Loving Yourself

Loving yourself and others protects the people around us from becoming culprits, and us from taking on the victim's role, even if we'll have to deal with anger, irritation and accusations. Love makes us take on responsibility for ourselves and stops us from burdening others with it. The miracle of love is that it is new every day and you never know what it will decide on next. A minute ago I thought I had to say 'no' for the sake of truth and love. But on taking a few breaths deep into my heart, there is now room for another, higher truth to unfold and for a truly different 'yes' to emerge. This time though, a genuine 'yes' replaces the fearful 'yes'. This is so much better for everybody.

The Self-love Test

We didn't put this self-love test right at the beginning of the book for a reason. We were hoping that the results would already look a bit more positive after all the exercises in the first part of the book. After all, we want to give ourselves courage with this book.

This test is certainly not comprehensive, but it is supposed to give you a general idea of how your love for yourself is doing so far. For each question, choose the answer that best represents your feelings.

1. How was last week for you?

A. I had a wonderful week, even when I was on the train, only friendly and happily smiling people sat next to me. My co-workers were mostly nice and helpful, and there is much light and love in this world.

B. As you sow, so shall you reap. When I seem to have been seeing only grumpy faces for a while, I checked my own inner attitude and once I'd done that, others started being nicer right away. Last week, I managed to do this, at least to a certain extent.

C. The people around me were all in a terrible mood. They either ignored me or were impolite and irritated. At work there's lots of bullying going on, again. And even my partner used to show much more affection than nowadays.

♥ ♥ ♥ ♥

2. ***You are at a party and start talking to someone you don't know. When you mention your name, he says: 'Ah, I've heard so much about you.' What are your thoughts on hearing that?***

A. How nice, then he must have heard lots of nice things about me.

B. Who cares who told whom what, now we'll see anyway if we like each other or not.

C. Uhuh, that can't have been good, he must have a terrible opinion of me.

❤❤❤❤

3. ***Are you able to sit in a café and have a drink on your own?***

   A. What a question, of course I am! It does happen every now and then, when I'm travelling. I love the flair of foreign places and sitting in a café by myself, watching everything that is going on around me.

   B. If I have to, I can, but I don't feel very comfortable doing anything like that.

   C. Dear goodness, no, I wouldn't even know what to do with myself there, all on my own.

❤❤❤❤

4. ***Let's assume you've forgotten the birthday of a close relative, whom you've always remembered to call. What do you think about yourself?***

   A. It could have happened to anyone, I'll just send her the warmest and heartfelt, if belated, birthday wishes now. She'll understand anyway, that it has nothing to do with how much I love her.

   B. Oh dear, I've recently realized that I keep forgetting more and more things, just what is wrong with me? Of course, I'll call and apologize and tell her how awful I feel.

C. I'm such an idiot, that'll put me in such a bad light! The whole family will get at me and I'm the black sheep anyway.

♥♥♥♥

5. ***Let's assume a close relative of yours, who usually remembers your birthday, didn't call this year. What's your conclusion?***

A. He must have forgotten, it happens to everyone. If I miss hearing his voice, I'll call him over the next few days and get myself a belated 'Happy Birthday'. I can already see us laughing about this next time we speak.

B. I forgive him, I'm sure he didn't mean any harm. I find it much easier to be lenient with other people's mistakes than with my own anyway. If the tables were turned and it was me who forgot his birthday, I'd feel worse. What counts is that I didn't do anything wrong. Him I can forgive.

C. That's impossible, I know him. This can only mean that he is upset with me, or that everyone in the family's been gossiping about me, and now everyone will turn their back on me.

♥♥♥♥

6. ***A notoriously bad-tempered person shouts at you in front of everyone, making unjustified accusations. How does this make you feel?***

   A. Everyone knows that those who shout the loudest have the most to hide. That'll just make him unpopular with everyone; I'm above such things.

   B. I hope the others also know that can't be right, and I glance around looking for help.

   C. I immediately panic and feel guilty. That is my natural reaction, no matter whether I am actually guilty or not. I often feel like I've done something wrong.

◘ ◘ ◘ ◘

7. ***Your job keeps you really busy at the moment and you are about to finish an urgent task. One of your colleagues comes up to you and asks you to help him with something important right away. What's your answer?***

   A. 'Sorry, I don't have time just at the moment. On the contrary, I could do with a bit of help myself right now. Please look for someone else to help you out.' The demanding tone alone makes you feel less and less inclined to help, even if you had the time.

B. You feel undecided and wonder if between the two of you there is a balance between giving and receiving. If so, you ask him first what it is about before deciding whether or not to put your own stuff aside to help him.

C. You have never been able to turn someone down, even if this gets you into trouble. You drop everything and agree to help with a heavy heart.

♥ ♥ ♥ ♥

8. ***Someone compliments you on your outfit. What's your reaction?***

A. 'Thanks, that is very kind of you.'

B. 'Thanks, it really isn't special, it was quite cheap.'

C. 'Ah, this old rag…'

♥ ♥ ♥ ♥

9. ***You are sitting in a café with two friends, having a lively chat. After a while, the conversation dies, and nobody says anything for a while. What do you think?***

A. Nice to be able to just sit here and relax, all three of us, without having to talk all the time.

B. The situation makes me feel uncomfortable. I manage a smile and hope someone will just say something as soon as possible.

C. Something like that always makes me feel totally embarrassed. I immediately start to rack my brain for something to say, to stop the silence. I feel responsible for the other people's feelings and don't want them to think that I feel bored in their company.

♥ ♥ ♥ ♥

10. You go on a holiday with a group of friends and have split the chores between you. How fair are you?

A. I contribute my part and want everything to be fair, but without causing any stress. It doesn't have to be super precise. However, if there's something I really dislike doing, I'll always try to swap with someone who maybe prefers my chore to his or her own. For instance, I prefer washing up to drying up. I like to make things as comfortable as possible for myself.

B. I pay very close attention to doing precisely the amount I am supposed to, neither more nor less. I wouldn't like to feel exploited, nor would I like other people to speak ill of me. I make sure that everyone notices me doing my part.

C. I love the feeling of being needed and important. In such situations I usually do more than others, so everyone must feel grateful.

Evaluation

When it comes to loving yourself, the more As you ticked, the better, the more Bs, the more mediocre, and the more Cs, the farther away your are from loving yourself. In case you have used this test as an excuse to give yourself a good roasting again, true to the motto: 'Oh dear, I've ticked so many Cs, I'm just so stupid…', then have some of your friends and colleagues do the test and ask them how many As they got. You'll see, most people struggle with quite similar issues. If you start to think and react more towards option A when you are in situations similar to those above, it will be a bit as if the frog managed to kiss itself to break the spell. And once you are the prince or princess, many will be more than happy to take you as an example and start to leave their froggy existence behind. Or simply try the 'Self-love Mantra'!

'The most terrifying thing is to accept oneself completely.'

Carl Jung

Exercise

The Self-love Mantra is as easy as it is effective. It goes like this: 'I love myself and allow others to love me'. Give it a try! Repeat this mantra in your mind as often as you can – at the bus stop, while cooking, tidying up and whenever you don't need to be concentrating on anything else. 'I love myself and allow others to love me.'

It's important to feel the meaning of the words, let the mantra flow into your heart, and then its full effect will unfold on the vibrations you send out. Others will notice this and feel drawn to you, and you will feel better about yourself. Repeat this exercise in your mind each day, on the train, while doing the dishes, while brushing your teeth… Let the mantra really soak into you.

Very often our love for ourselves is so heavily restricted that we mistrust people who want to love us. We don't allow them to do so, because we think, 'They can't really love me, I don't deserve such love…'

'I allow myself to be loved' doesn't only refer to other people, but also to nature and the whole of creation. Allow yourself to be loved by everything. When you are able to permit this completely, you will automatically feel at one with everything. The pot of love inside you will overflow and your love will flow back.

The continuation of the mantra then comes very naturally: 'I am love and I love to give love'. I only have more to give away, when I have more myself. So loving yourself, therefore, comes before giving love away. Anybody who feels empty inside won't be capable of giving away very much. But maybe a little sabotaging voice still whispers inside you, 'Oh, but I am not really worth much, am I? Who could possibly want my love anyway…?' If, on the other hand, you enjoy loving yourself, you will also automatically enjoy giving love away.

Here's another option. Imagine that you are love and you give some of it away, and all of the love that you give automatically flows back to you from the cosmos multiplied many times. You can also practise both exercises in parallel. Explore what suits you best, and what is happening inside you.

Tip

Do not destroy the effect of the mantra with the pressure of expectations. Practise first and foremost in order to give yourself something. The wish for other people to give you love only develops once you have 'satiated yourself with love'.

A friend of mine repeated this mantra again and again in her thoughts for a whole week. She wanted to test out its effect on her marriage. The first to react was her six-year-old daughter. The child likes to be cuddled and hugged, but neither wants to be kissed, nor has ever given her mother a kiss, and she had also never said 'I love you' to her mother, either.

After her mother had used the mantra for a whole week, her daughter rushed up to her suddenly and cried out: 'Mama, I love you sooooooo much', and planted kisses up and down her mother's arm – and the expression on her face while she was doing so was a picture. This had never happened before. Her mother was completely amazed by the mantra's powerful effect.

The Miracle of Loving Yourself

Over time, many mothers and fathers of 'cool' teenagers have tried out this exercise and have sent us truly wonderful feedback about it. Many of the teenagers suddenly became less cool. Mum and Dad were given hugs again and even given the occasional kiss. Or the teens suddenly began to trust their parents again with more of their feelings. These kinds of exercises can have a truly miraculous effect. Although one doesn't say or do anything that is noticeable to the people around, the effect on them is huge.

Part 2

Loving Yourself for Expert Practitioners

Complain or Value?

The first question in the self-love test on page 51 is one that shows you how much self-love you are sending out on an unconscious level. Have you ever noticed, for example, that some people find something to complain and moan about in every situation and with every person? The weather today is too hot, tomorrow it's too wet, the food today is too salty, and tomorrow too fatty. These kinds of people always find something that isn't good and isn't right. In the language of love, these people are saying, 'I don't love the weather. Neither today nor tomorrow. The weather is just always bad, however it is at the moment – and it keeps changing, too! And I don't love food. And anyway I don't love anything: politics, my tax return, my football club, my boss, my work, my neighbours', and so on.

If we are being precise, you have to say that this type of person not only doesn't love the weather but also actually rejects it: 'So, the weather we had today, I don't like it at all. I reject this weather; I want different weather, now, immediately.' If you think about this kind of person, someone who always complains and moans, how do you think they feel inside? Maybe you have a colleague like this, someone you always meet at the Christmas party. Or an uncle who always behaves like this. Feel your way inside them, how do you think they are doing? Honestly?

Maybe you find being with them somehow uncomfortable. A gust of dissatisfaction and disapproval always seem to waft into the room as soon as they appear. It is almost like the storm that threatens at the end of a summer's day. In Bavaria, you call this type of person 'dour'. Not the sort of person you want to spend time with. Why is this actually so? The world around us is a reflection of the world inside. If I always judge everything around me to be bad, wrong and terrible, then it is only an expression of the state within me. Then I can't be doing well internally either. If I reject and disparage many of the things around me, then in that moment, I am doing exactly the same to myself internally. I am doing myself down. I reject myself, or parts of myself. I do not love myself. Complaining and being bad-tempered are symptoms of a lack of self-love, just as coughing and sniffing are symptoms of a cold.

The conclusion is crystal clear, that praise, recognition and value are an expression of self-love. If the world around me is just a reflection of the world inside me, then everything that I recognize to be good and beautiful is a reflection of my own inner beauty and growing love for myself. And so we come to the great exercise in loving yourself.

Exercise

The world around you reflects the world within you. The more conscious you become, the more certain you will be of the beauty of the world around you. It will become an expression of your own inner beauty. Collect the beauty, the approaches of others and the love from the world that surrounds you, just as a bee collects pollen from a flower, individually, grain by grain. Go through your day and collect the pleasant incidents in your honeypot.

- Each smile that you encounter is an expression of your love for yourself.
- Each time that you receive praise is an expression of love.
- When a person is friendly to you, it is an expression of love.
- When a dog comes up to you joyfully to sniff you, it is love.
- When the sun shines, it is love.
- When you encounter a happy person, it is a sign of the love that surrounds you.

- A flower by the wayside is a sign that the cosmos loves you. The same applies to a rainbow, a hot meal or your faithful car, which is always happy to drive you wherever you want to go.

Make a list for yourself in which you collect and record the many ways that love plays around you each day. This list will focus your attention on love and thankfulness, and strengthen your love for yourself. Make it your aim to discover at least one new expression of love in the world around you each day. Play this game while driving your car, waiting for the train, or going for a walk. Then keep reminding yourself about what you have discovered. Make a habit of seeing the world in this way.

The Miracle of Loving Yourself

If you do this exercise often you won't be able to avoid becoming aware of your own beauty. Your love for yourself will grow, also merely because you value the world around you more and consciously pay more attention to it. Beauty lies everywhere, and is waiting for you to discover it.

See the Love Inside Every Single Person

♥♥♥♥

The last chapter reminded us that the world around us is simply a reflection of the world within us. Whatever I reject in others, I either fear or reject within myself. If, on the other hand, we search for the love within others, we can also increase our level of self-love. We can learn to recognize myriad forms of love expressing themselves in other people – and so to recognize these within ourselves as well, even in difficult situations.

A few flashes of insight from a seminar can illustrate this:

- 'As I was waiting at the train station on my way here, I saw an extremely fat and somewhat dishevelled-looking woman. She was listening to her mobile with a hangdog expression. I clearly rejected her. On reflection I understood that she too was yearning for love – the same as me. Maybe her date hadn't arrived and wasn't answering the phone. Now I feel sorry for her and wish her lots of love and happiness.'

- 'Until just now I have been internally rejecting a woman here in this group. But now her hidden 'cry for love' is very obvious to me. I can't understand now why I didn't recognize it immediately, and why I was so offhand with her instead. When I feel my way into the situation more carefully, I realize that I actually had a poor opinion of myself at that moment, which I simply transferred to the woman.'
- 'The caretaker snapped at me a short time ago, when I asked him for a blanket, although there was a whole pile of them in the corner that I hadn't seen. He certainly wasn't filled with love at that moment. Maybe he has a lot to do right now and was feeling tired. His bad mood wasn't aimed at me (not even if that was his intention). He simply lacked love and happiness just then.'
- 'As H. came into the room, I asked myself what he was doing at a seminar like this. He was looking around himself in such a cool and emotionless way that I just couldn't understand it. Then I asked myself how love might express itself within him. And I had the idea that he might be good at mediating conflicts because he was able to gain a perspective by keeping his distance, while others become completely involved. I asked H., and he said that this was his

profession. He taught non-aggressive communication for mediating conflicts. It is amazing, with love in your heart, how much you are able to perceive what was hidden from you beforehand!'

- 'What I enjoy most is going round and gazing into the eyes of people and searching for the 'kernel of love' within each pair of eyes. You can see it in some people immediately, if you are in resonance with them, and in other pairs of eyes you have to search more deeply. I find this exhilarating. I just have to stop myself from staring into people's eyes too penetratingly in my everyday life…'

Exercise

You can do this exercise with each and every person you encounter. See the love within them. Find your own way. For example, you can:

- Keep a look out for the kernel of love in their eyes.
- Ask yourself how the love within this person might be expressed. This doesn't mean that you have to discover this person's true talent, but rather imagine how this person might express their love.
- Recognize the wish for love within this person.
- Recognize the cry for love (which is often expressed negatively).

- Look closely to see whether this person is driven more by fear or love, or a mixture of the two.
- Think about how much self-love this person is showing at the moment.

And, by the way, what does your level of self-love look like at the moment? What percentage of self-love do you estimate you have right now? Remember it can change from hour to hour. If your level should be low at the moment, I recommend that you repeat the following mantra to yourself in your thoughts: 'I love myself and see love everywhere'. This is also a wonderful mantra to guide you on a day when you plan to see the love within everybody.

The Miracle of Loving Yourself

The more you are able to see the various forms of love expressed in the most diverse people, the stronger, deeper and more comprehensive your love for yourself will become. Being able to see love all around you will strengthen your love for yourself. You automatically see yourself as being worthy of love when you are able to perceive love even in the most difficult of people.

'Once we're thrown off our habitual paths, we think all is lost, but it's only here that the new and the good begins.'

Leo N. Tolstoy

Change Your Thought Patterns

♥♥♥♥

My healer recently gave me the following piece of advice: 'Always make sure that whatever you do doesn't use up more of your energy than you get in return. Always be mindful of your inner balance in everything that you do.' I found this very interesting. As a matter of fact, it never occurred to me that even the kind of things that usually keep me busy during the day (including cleaning, tidying up and book-keeping) could give me energy in the first place, even if I do try what I can to make the best out of it. My healer, though, looks at it from a different angle – and he's right! There are possibilities for us to take care of tasks we feel are unpleasant to begin with in such a way that they give us energy. For example, there is 'Zen-cleaning', a meditatively concentrated approach to tidying up, that involves inner presence and gratitude for the things we tidy up, or an approach to book-keeping, which is full of fascination for the interesting receipts and the stories they have to tell. If we managed to do that, then everything we do would also give us energy. We would always be in perfect balance, relaxed and happy, and we would never feel exhausted.

So all it would take to make this dream come true is for us merely to change our habits? Experts used to assume that our personality had developed fully by the age of 35 and that the thought patterns we have established by then can hardly be changed. Today, modern researchers into neuroscience such as Gerald Hüther or Joe Dispenza have found that even at the age of 150 the brain would still be capable of changing its patterns and structures completely – and that is mostly thanks to willpower. Joe Dispenza has conducted some interesting research on this. When showing a bunch of pictures to a group of depressed people, with 50 per cent of the pictures depicting a funeral and the other 50 per cent a wedding, the participants were afterwards convinced that they had seen more funeral pictures. This is because gloomy people are wired in such a way that they don't recognize positive things, even if they're staring them in the face. They only pay attention to what's negative, as this is what dominates their thoughts. If, however, you conduct the same experiment with a group of happy people, they will be convinced they have seen more wedding pictures.

Think bigger!

This is because every thought of yours activates a messenger substance in your body, which then induces an emotion. This feeling then supports the thought you had, which, in turn, activates the corresponding messenger substance, and so on. This mechanism of thought-messenger substance-feeling is constantly repeated, so that a think–feel–think habit forms that not only sustains itself but creates a pattern which etches itself through your entire body. This pattern then causes similar situations to happen in your life over and over again. However, according to Dispenza, we can escape this mechanism by consciously 'thinking bigger' than the current situation suggests. For example, people who go on whining and complaining in their minds about how awful everything is, keep themselves caught up in the situation. If, however, you manage to focus your attention on the positive things in life instead, and imagine that everything can take a turn for the better at any moment, because there are good people and opportunities wherever you look, you will mentally outgrow the situation and think bigger. As a result, new messenger substances form as well as new feelings, which then bring about new thoughts. In this way, our brain can rewire itself.

For this to work, we have to use our willpower, because there's this one problem. In most cases we've been thinking in these rigid ways for decades. Our body won't just give up craving the food it's become used to (messenger substances), it will interfere, supported by our weaker self: 'Oh come on, putting those new thoughts aside until tomorrow will be just fine…' As a matter of fact, our weaker self is addicted to our body's old established messenger substances. Only a strict diet and abstinence from our unwholesome old thoughts can help now.

Exercise

No matter whether there is a reason at hand, or none in sight, just be happy! It always gets easier after a bit of practice. Ask yourself: 'How would I feel, how would I move, how would I hold myself, what would I do, if I were super-happy about something right now?' Unfold your talent as an actor and act out a feeling of pure happiness. I'm best doing this in front of my bathroom mirror. My children give me bewildered looks every time they catch me doing this, but I suppose you can get used to everything, even to a crazy mum.

'Where's mum?'

'She's in the bathroom, making faces in front of the mirror again…' 'Oh, I see…'

View the messenger substances as your audience. The sooner they start to change and cause genuine feelings of happiness (even if, at the beginning, they are just flashes of happiness and dissipate again quickly), the better your performance. If nothing changes, you'll need to put on a more convincing act. The messenger substances couldn't care less whether or not there is an actual reason for your happiness. If they buy it, they'll simply do their job, without even taking a look at what's happening in the outside world. And if you've really mastered the exercise, the feeling of happiness will last for hours.

Tip

Collect small pebbles or something similar and put a handful of them into your left pocket in the morning. Every time you experience something positive, take one out and put it into your right pocket. If you only wear skirts without pockets, you can always use two little lunch bags instead. Mark them so you can distinguish one from another and carry them with you in your handbag, backpack or whatever works best for you. Be creative. In the evening, check how many pebbles have switched bags, and think back about each positive incident you've come across during the day.

Now you can start to feel happy again, and this time you have a reason. There are various reasons for 'happy-stones'. You had a pleasant conversation, or a friendly encounter, you did something well, you are pleased with a decision, you got to enjoy the sun, you did something a bit better than you used to, you had a great idea... Anything goes, so long as you stop collecting 'misery-stones', like most people do, which remind you of everything that went badly. If you carry and move happy-stones around, you'll reprogramme your brain to love much faster.

Discover new sources of energy

Many spiritual schools of thought prompt their students to constantly ask themselves the following question: 'What gives me energy, what depletes my energy?' These are good questions to start with, but it doesn't automatically mean that you shouldn't touch anything that might deplete your energy. 'Filing paperwork for my boss uses up my energy, I'll just go ahead and palm it off on someone else. Eating chocolate and drinking lots of coffee give me energy, so let's have some more of that.' Naturally it's not that simple.

In a lot of cases, it's not actually so much about changing what I do, but how I do it and what mental attitude I have while doing it. How can I make myself feel comfortable in a way that even filing gives me energy? What positive effects can I glean from doing it? How can I reward myself afterwards? Maybe by going for a walk?

Eating chocolate only satisfies in the short term and doesn't do the body any good in the long run. What's my ravenous appetite trying to tell me? What is it I'm really starving for? What could give me satisfaction in the long run? What do I need right now? How can I give it to myself? The answer might be to call a good friend, a date for tonight, or looking forward to a relaxing bath, to name but a few.

Exercise

Ask yourself the following questions: What gives me energy, what uses up my energy? What could I possibly change to get more energy from what I'm doing right now? Anything can supply us with energy, if we develop our appreciation for the little, everyday things in life.

Don't let happy moments pass you by

Let me tell you a pretty little story:

John-I-really-can't-stand-myself from the Dissatisfaction tribe has got a job, a wife, kids, a house, a new car and is relatively healthy. He still finds his life dull and unsatisfactory. His boss doesn't quite understand his genius, the people at work are useless anyway, his wife annoys him, not to speak of the children, the car could've been cheaper, and his doctor is an idiot who hasn't managed to cure even the smallest attack of gout.

One day, his cousin Jim-I-love-myself-a-lot comes over. The guy is such a pain in the neck. John has never liked him. But today, something unexpected happens. Jim tells him about his life: his wife has left him, the business went bankrupt and he has to move to a smaller apartment. Jim is sad, but has some comfort because the neighbour's cat has decided to come over for a cuddle three times a day. Jim has noticed how much happiness he gets out of stroking the cat with all his heart. If he does that, everything seems to be a bit less grim, and he looks towards the future with more confidence.

Suddenly, it strikes John that his life has been a series of missed opportunities to be happy. The penny drops, and from this moment onwards, he is a happy person. He never again has the same ungrateful and careless thoughts. The fact that, within a blink of an eye, his whole life was elevated to a new level, is a story written in a different book and should be told another time.

Exercise

Make yourself aware of the small, happy moments, too. In your mind, take a microscope, pay attention and examine every little moment of happiness, however small it may be. This will also help you to reprogramme your brain!

As with every exercise, this also requires willpower. But the more exercises in loving yourself you do, the higher your self-esteem and the easier you will find it to do something for yourself. Never ask yourself, 'Which exercise am I going to force myself to do next?', but rather, 'Which exercise can I do at the moment that will be fun and will make me feel really good afterwards?'.

♡♥♡

The Miracle of Loving Yourself

The more often you can rejoice in tiny things for no apparent reason, the greater the miracle of your transformation will be! The feeling of happiness is the one that overwrites old patterns most quickly. Once you've been feeling really happy for a while in situations you used to despise, the old behavioural pattern will be gone and not return, no matter how many decades it had been lording it on its throne. Within a couple of weeks you can reverse everything, if you put your heart and soul in it. Sweep the misery-stones from the throne and put the happy-stones in their place. Your life will become a series of happy moments you have seized.

Loving Yourself Requires Time, So Do Relationships

According to a report by *Focus* magazine, one reason for the alleged 'end of love' in society is the acceleration occurring in all areas of life, as well as increasing job and career changes. If you constantly change your job, and therefore probably where you live, sustaining long-term relationships becomes a challenge. Staying in touch with friends is taking a faster pace as well, as having easy chats online is so much quicker than actually going to a café to meet up. Many people even brush their teeth faster than they used to, eat faster, get changed faster, take showers faster and so on. We are under the impression that we must save as much time as possible. But why, exactly? According to statistics, we spend more time watching TV or in front of a computer. Have we gone completely mad?

No wonder love doesn't really seem to fit into this fast-moving environment. Love requires time, a lot of time actually, to look closely, to take note of all the details and to revel in them. In order to appreciate and love a person, taking a brief glance to establish what colour their eyes are just won't do. You need to delve into their personality, to understand, and to look really closely. Love emerges when you take time to explore another person.

This is as true for the love you have for another person as it is for the love you have for yourself. The latter might even require a particularly long time, as we are not used to examining ourselves in all our emotional nuances anymore. For that matter, when was the last time that you fully enjoyed examining your feelings, and putting your finger precisely on what is going on inside you while, for instance, standing by a tree or a lake?

The desire for healing

Anyone who takes the time to get to know themself will also be confronted with their own shady sides and neuroses. Whether we attempt to cure them, or to accept them the way they are, is not the decisive factor. The bottom line is that we need to truly know ourselves and our special characteristics to be able to love ourselves and be happy with the way we are. The power of loving yourself is also contagious and has a healing effect on your partner, who automatically meets with more empathy and understanding from a 'love-person' who is able to recognize the internal distress causing certain behaviour. This even works with someone whose communication is determined by fear, who is trapped in that fear and can't see love. Even this kind of 'fear-person' will react differently to an understanding 'love-person' than to representatives of their own type, who are unfriendly as well, or only see the weaknesses in other people (so that they don't have to examine their own, which scare them). Therefore, a relationship works in totally different ways, depending on what combination of people gets together.

Fear-person meets fear-person

Partner A asks a normal question. Partner B reacts with fear and thinks: 'Uhuh, he wants to offend me…' and answers back rudely. A gets angry, B even more so, a huge fight ensues, followed by separation, and the next partner. Everything begins all over again, with no significant change. Both partners end up bolstering each other's downsides and neuroses more than anything else.

Fear-person meets love-person

Partner A asks a normal question. Partner B reacts with fear and thinks: 'Uhuh, she must be trying to offend me…', and answers back rudely. A recognizes the fear behind this behaviour and reacts with empathy and self-love. That means that A distances herself, but in a loving way, without shutting the other person out, while not shying away either, but looking after herself instead. B's anger will fade away relatively quickly, depending on the degree and depth of fear. A doesn't let any of this unsettle her and remains firm in her love for herself, and soon after that, everything looks rosy again.

Love-person meets love-person

Partner A is in a bad mood and asks a question with a cynical undertone. Partner B draws breath, feels into herself and replies as follows: 'This tone makes me feel offended and automatically makes me feel guilty. I feel as if I don't even know what this is really about. Is there another problem I should know of?' A realizes that he has taken out his bad mood on B, reflects, and answers: 'My colleague spoke ill of me in front of our boss today, which left me feeling very frustrated. I think my question incorporated some vibrations of my anger, I'm sorry. What I actually meant to ask is…'

♥ ♥ ♥ ♥

The last example shows how every problem that arises is also an opportunity to bring both partners more healing, help them to become mentally freer, more affectionate and happier. But things like this require time – first and foremost for loving yourself. Only those who know their feelings in particular situations are also able to understand others when they say one thing, but mean another.

‘All genesis in nature, in humans, in love must wait, be patient, until the time comes for it to blossom.’

DIETRICH BONHOEFFER

Exercise

Every time someone asks you a question or says something that evokes unpleasant feelings in you, note down the situation and, as soon as possible, take time to explore yourself. What is it that I disliked about it and why? What effects did it have on me? You might not be able to find a feeling inside yourself right from the start, but the more you examine and look at your feelings, the easier it will get, and in many situations your anger will automatically be transformed into understanding and sympathy. This is because if you truly understand yourself, you'll also understand others better.

Let me give you an example. A colleague asks you if you like your current job. This set off alarm bells in your head. Here are a few of the countless possible reasons for your reaction:

- You were afraid that the subtext of what your colleague was saying was that he is better than you.
- You had no faith in your own judgement and didn't want to show any weakness by giving a stupid answer.
- You thought he wanted to be praised and sweet-talked, and if you told him the truth he'd start bullying you.

Our inner fears can come up with plenty of peculiar thoughts like these in reaction to a simple question. The more precisely we perceive and understand them, the better we get to know ourselves. By the way, the same works for our positive feelings. When a statement or a conversation has been particularly good for you, examine your feelings towards it as well. What was it, exactly, that gave you such a good feeling? How can you get more of this feeling? Can you give it to other people, too?

Let the love for yourself grow by taking more time for the things that are really important to you. Get rid of the many things in your life that don't actually give you satisfaction.

The Miracle of Loving Yourself

Those who love more are loved more in return. Set yourself the objective that the people you meet go away a little bit happier than they were before they came to you. Wonderful things can happen. Sometimes, people you thought were hopeless cases will start to change their behaviour towards you. Suddenly, they are positive towards you and, out of the blue, give you back many times over what you have given them. This can be just like a big miracle. It might not always work out, but the intention alone will strengthen your love for yourself and sensitize your perception of feelings. Take time for these little things in life, they can work wonders. Love likes slowness and only unfolds when you really make room for it, in yourself and in your life. The miracle of consciously enjoying slowness lies in its ability to enrich your life very rapidly and make your life feel more satisfied and fulfilled.

How Do You Treat Yourself?

This is one of the chapters that I write mostly for myself. As a matter of fact, this topic always makes me take a good look at myself. A lovely acquaintance of mine recently told me about an incident that occurred when he was a student at university. A doctor he knew gave him a book with the following dedication: 'Be tough on yourself and brutal to others. With best regards, PhD, KM.' Back then he was incredibly appalled at such a dedication. In the meantime, he has been working as a doctor himself for many years and knows this type of person quite well from his practice. It's the kind of person who gets up at seven in the morning to go running, calls the first staff meeting at eight to rub everybody's noses in the fact that they are all slowcoaches and have only just got out of bed. Next, a tight schedule for the day is set, eating is only acceptable if there's a possibility to combine it with a business meeting, and everyone leaving work on time is obviously a loser.

I have no employees and therefore don't have to go running at seven in the morning – after all, there is not anyone's nose that I could rub in it. No, I'm just joking, of course. It's not actually about running after all, but about the fact that he quite obviously doesn't like it and takes out his frustration about it on others. He is being tough on himself and brutal to others. The boss could equally go running out of love for himself and arrange a 15 minutes running or yoga break before the morning meeting – and simultaneously do away with overtime at work, of course. In this way he would treat himself and his employees lovingly, which is much more fun and healthier too.

Tough body – tough mind

In the past, a really long time ago, basically almost in a past life of mine (to be precise until a few months ago) I was just like that. Everything was so exciting and constantly short of time, I would always do just this one last thing really, really quickly and then swiftly yet another one. Grant yourself just one little hour of sleep less, eat a bit more quickly and skip going for a walk, then you might just get even more done. People, however, aren't only made up of a restless mind that is easily excitable, there's also a body attached that needs to support everything we do. If I treat myself toughly in this, or similar ways, by not really granting

'We ought to fear a man who hates himself; for we are liable to become the victims of his anger and revenge. Let us therefore try to tempt him into self-love.'

Friedrich Nietzsche

myself the breaks I need to keep my inner balance, my body will become tough, too. Body, mind and soul form an entity, and each level reflects what is happening on the other two. When the body gets hard, the body cells turn, metaphorically speaking, from grapes into raisins, they dry out, there isn't enough vital juice and energy. You can't let go, either mentally or emotionally, and this is transferred onto the body. I was in it up to my neck, and know that millions of people do more or less the same.

Losing balance

If this state continues for a longer period, you will face physical, mental and emotional problems. The cells and tissues become matted and clogged; the microcirculation in the cells is impaired. The body has difficulties in sending oxygen and white blood cells into every corner of the body, which leads to pain and illnesses. The same happens to the mind. Your thoughts become matted and clog up. You are less and less able to think clearly, creatively and flexibly. Instead, your brain is stuck on repeat like a broken record, and it gets increasingly harder to free yourself from automatic behaviour and unpleasant thought patterns, as they are equally stuck in their ways.

With everything being connected, we can easily reverse this process from the physical level. As soon as the energy starts flowing more freely again through the body, the mind will notice the effects and feel freer as well. If we then proceed on to the mental and emotional level and start working on our self-love and inner freedom, the levels will support and speed each other up.

On the physical level it is quite simple to restore tissue elasticity. It is achieved through muscle tremors, as the trembling causes clotted cells to loosen up. The trembling also re-establishes the body's natural rhythm, in which the fluids pulsate through it as normal. The so-called matrix-rhythm-therapy is a kind of 'trembling-deep-tissue-massage', which re-stimulates the cells' microcirculation. But you can also do it completely for free by yourself – it takes a bit longer, but is just as effective.

Exercise

You can try several trembling exercises to find out which ones you like:

- Lie down and flex your calves until they start to tremble. Then flex your body parts one by one, from bottom to top, until all your muscles tremble. Hold the tension only briefly, for as long as it's comfortable, and then relax. Important: don't put yourself under pressure to perform. On the contrary, as after all, what we want to achieve is reduced pressure. Do the exercise with playful curiosity towards the processes in your body. How does the trembling feel? How does it feel when you let it all go and trace the effects?

- Standing upright, gently sway and shake your entire body. While doing that, let your limbs hang loose, like jelly. If you are afraid of making mistakes, you can have a body therapist show you how the exercise works.
- There are mini-trampolines that you aren't supposed to jump on, but sway softly. Your feet never leave the trampoline. The swaying also helps the body to loosen up. It brings the lymph and all the body's energy back into flow and stimulates the blood circulation. Swaying for five minutes every day in the fresh air (or at an open window) is all you need to do to notice positive results.
- By the way, the massage heads in a warm thermal bath have a similar effect. Try and see for yourself, if you like this kind of thing! After such a shaking exercise, you can follow it with any self-love exercise or meditation to make optimum use of the increased energy flow. After shaking or rocking I like to go for a walk.

Unless Manfred comes along and we chat, I take every step consciously with this mantra: 'I love myself and I let go.' Then I examine where I'm still tense – in most cases around the shoulders, as I spend a lot of time sitting in front of a computer – and breathe deeply into that area. On repeating the mantra, the tense area relaxes. Try it for yourself; it is just so good for body, mind and also the soul!

Tip

Breathe in while rocking back and forth three times then breathe out while rocking five times. This brings additional calmness and placidity into your system. In addition, the combination with this breathing technique makes the lymph flow particularly well. Astronauts supposedly do this rocking-trampoline exercise, too.

So once more, just to make it absolutely clear: whether an exercise is effective or not doesn't depend on the exercise itself. Instead it depends on your attitude when doing the exercise. A mantra like 'I love myself and let go' just won't work for you at all, if you only reel it off. If, however, you can feel the love flow while doing the exercise, and pay close attention to the way it feels when you relax more and more, it will have the desired effect. It doesn't matter if you don't feel much at first. What counts is your genuine intention. Your soul will appreciate it, and your feeling and perception will become stronger and stronger over time.

Shake yourself free! Our natural state is to be happy and healthy, and to love and appreciate ourselves and everybody else the way we are. Shaking relieves our body, mind, and soul from ballast and thereby helps us to find this natural state.

The Miracle of Loving Yourself

If, at some point, you've shaken yourself properly free (provided you are physically fit enough for an extended trembling session) and relax and let your thoughts flow afterwards, the associations and daydreams that may arise will then show you very precisely where you are mentally and what inner patterns there still are to let go of. The physical shaking can also loosen up mental tightness. We have had seminars where these exercises reawakened memories in some participants that had been buried for decades. They had become ripe for 'plucking'. Every time something like that happens, it feels as if it's a miracle. On the surface, you've only shaken a few muscles but, in doing so, have managed to shake off some old patterns from your childhood as well. This is because our soul always loves us and would use any opportunity to free itself from old and useless stuff. However, such a change isn't usually as remarkable and spectacular as the one in the example above. In most cases, it sneaks in quietly through the back door instead, and all you notice is that you feel ever calmer and more relaxed. For someone who lives in constant stress, this can be a wonderfully relaxing and relieving experience.

How Do You Speak to Yourself?

♥♥♥♥

We often have African au pair girls from Nairobi staying with us. They frequently find the German weather quite unusual. The winter, of course, is too cold, but the summer – big surprise – is too warm for them. In Nairobi the sun rises later and goes down earlier than here. And if the temperature hits 30° Celsius for an hour then, to their minds, that was a hot day. If we have really hot weather, six hours of 35° Celsius aren't that unusual. The properly hot days are followed by equally muggy hot nights, while the nights in Nairobi are always cool. The girls are properly amazed, as they actually believe Kenya to be the hot country, not Germany.

Once we had a Kenyan au pair girl that hated the German weather, as she kept assuring me. It was too cold, too wet or too hot; there was always something to complain about. One day, however, the sky was blue and the temperature was a mild 20° Celsius. Finally, I thought. She must like the weather today. And you know what? That day, she thought the weather was boring.

This was when I realized that the weather was not the problem. The way she perceived the weather was just a reflection of her internal communication with herself. Even though she was a friendly, bubbly person in general and we all liked her, there were days when she couldn't stand herself. There was no point in trying to tell her about anything positive, because she felt everything about her was bad and was sure that her life made no sense, nobody loved her, and so forth. On these kinds of days, she wasn't bubbly, obviously.

Negative self-talk

In order to fathom the 'weather phenomenon', I launched a survey to find out how people usually communicate with themselves. This made me realize, in what an extremely unfriendly manner all of us talk to ourselves. Maybe, we adopted this habit during childhood or adolescence, when other people criticized us, our classmates made fun of us (to make themselves feel better and gloss over their own low self-esteem), and when the whole world seemed to be against us. Now it is high time for us to change this habit.

My survey went like this: 'When talking to yourself negatively, what is it you usually say, and how often do you say such things to yourself?' Here's a selection of the answers:

- I'm such an idiot.
- I'm useless.
- I'm an emotional cripple (many seem to think that).
- I'll never be able to do that.
- Everyone else can do it, but I'm just too stupid.
- That is too difficult for me. I'm sure everybody else is better than me. I am unlovable.
- I'll be alone forever, because I'm different from everybody else (that's a good one, as most people seem to think that of themselves – and always try to bond with people who are as poorly suited to them as possible, just so they can stick to their doctrine and end up alone again).
- I'm so silly; I've messed up again. I'll never learn!
- I say 'yes' even when I mean 'no', because I'm such a coward.
- I feel ashamed of myself that I'm so bad at taking decisions. Others can do it so well!
- I don't trust myself.

When asked about how often they have such a talk with themselves, people's answers were as follows: 'Well, actually there are several comments of that sort every day.' This is what we call negative self-hypnosis. Each thought naturally results in a feeling, which then seems to confirm the thought, and this process goes on and on in unhealthy, repeating and amplifying loops. When talking with good friends about their 'secret internal communication', you soon notice that everyone comes up with similar sentences. That has nothing to do with objectivity, but rather with fears and thinking habits. And we'll go ahead right now and change them on the spot.

Exercise

Make a list of how you would like to be. Note down the characteristic features and skills you would like to have. Here are a few examples:

- I would like to be confident in myself.
- I would like to believe in my strength.
- I would like to like myself.
- I would like to be courageous.
- I would like to be creative.
- I would like to be strong and friendly in any situation and believe in myself.
- I would like to love myself, including my flaws and weaknesses.

And now we do something incredibly easy (a friend of mine, who works as a coach, gave me this tip), we use the first wish on the list as an example. So let's assume that you would like to have confidence in yourself. On a scale from one to ten (saying zero is not an option!), how much confidence would you estimate you already have in yourself? Let's assume you'd give yourself two points for confidence in yourself. Then note down all the things that are good already, which made you realize that your self-confidence already lies at two on the scale. Keep a look out for the positive things and reinforce them by making yourself aware of them.

Once you've noted everything down, think about what you would need or have to do, to get one more point (in this case, three). Then do the same for all the desired characteristics or skills on your list. This leaves you with a wonderful list of all the things you can do and are good at.

Changing statements about yourself

Use this list as a basis for changing the way you communicate with yourself. Observe yourself. Whenever you notice you're communicating with yourself in an unfriendly manner, think about ways to change this. Imagine you were your own child and wanted to raise yourself to be a confident, positive-thinking person. How would you talk to yourself?

Let me give you a few examples.

- 'I'm such an idiot.' New thought: 'So what, I still love myself.' Find a pet name for yourself. Every time you think 'idiot', change it to this: 'That's not true at all, honey (or sweetie), I love myself!'
- 'I'm useless.' New thought: 'I'm very able. I'm already capable of doing many things. Wouldn't it just be boring if there weren't anything to improve? I love myself the way I am.'
- 'I'm an emotional cripple.' New thought: 'How would I like to be when my love for myself and my love for others remain in balance? I know I am already a bit like that. I am already good at this and that…'
- 'I'll never be able to do that.' New thought: 'It took Thomas Edison 10,000 attempts to get his invention of the light bulb to shine. I can do anything as well, as long as I really want it.'
- 'I'm a bad mother (or father).' Such thoughts have never resulted in a better mother or father. There must be many things you've done well. Even if you can't think of anything right now, try thinking like this: 'I'm a good mother (a good father).' Maybe the new sentence will relax you so much, that as a result

you'll be able to let more love flow towards your children and stop beating yourself up all the time.

This is something you can always do anyway. Just think the opposite of the former sentence and pay attention to what happens to your feelings. Thinking the same thought often enough means that it becomes a part of us, and our subconscious believes it. Even the biggest grouch gets into a better mood when thinking this of himself: 'In reality, I am the world's brightest little Mr Sunshine!'

Observe the changes that happen to your feelings. Experiment with yourself. Which thoughts about yourself are especially good for you?

The healing effect of good thoughts

The neuroscientist Joe Dispenza interviewed people who had been cured spontaneously from an allegedly incurable illness. All participants had decided from one day to the next to become a new person and never ever to think the same destructive thoughts again. They all realized that they'd become ill because of their way of reacting to their environment. They didn't become ill because someone else treated them badly, but because they had been thinking badly about themselves. They didn't become ill because someone else shouted at them, but because they reacted with fear and panic. 'Not anymore', they decided and, from that point onwards, started to think in completely new ways. Their motivation was inspired by their position on the edge of a cliff. They remained constant and returned back to health.

Build up your own positive communication with yourself. Take a look at your thoughts and start talking in a friendly way to yourself from today. If you need encouragement, refer back to your notes to see what you can do and what you're good at. With some willpower and an attitude that you are worth it, you can begin to talk to yourself affectionately, starting from today.

The Miracle of Loving Yourself

A course participant who had severe health issues before starting the exercise had her doubts: 'But if I don't think my usual thoughts ever again, then I won't be myself anymore.' Soon after, however, she said: 'Wow, I'm still myself. But I have become the best part of myself. From what I know now I can say, that I've actually known all along that I contained all this beauty and love within me, but I couldn't find a way to let them out and live through them. Now I talk kindly to myself and others and feel much closer to myself than ever before. I perceive my emotions much better now. I used to be a stranger to myself!'

Slow Wish-fulfilment

♥♥♥♥

We live in fast times, so let's start with the fast wishes. When I place an order with the cosmos and it's delivered by return, I immediately get the feeling that the cosmos has really listened and reacted. I feel full of euphoria and excitement; it's just so much fun. I particularly love it when I need a birthday present for someone really urgently, or acutely require a hint or a pressing solution. In such cases I'm always very grateful for a prompt delivery.

While a friend of mine was on his way to a business meeting, his GPS system broke down. Naturally, he didn't have a map because, being a modern person, he blindly put all his trust in technology. At the next traffic light, he begged the cosmos to get his GPS going again. The couple in the car next to him couldn't help but noticing and had to laugh. They asked if he needed any help and, without hesitating, gave him their old city map – they'd just bought a new, more up-to-date one a couple of days ago and hadn't thrown the old one away yet. The cosmos had carried out delivery, not as expected, but fair enough. In such cases, we usually need a quick helping hand, if possible, right away. However, in some situations a prompt fulfilment of our wish can become a punishment, even if that sounds incredibly unlikely. Let me give you an impressive example:

Easy money can come and go easily

One of my readers, who runs a small business, wrote a letter to me about his cosmic order. He'd been heavily in debt and unceremoniously ordered several million euros from the cosmos. Incredibly, they were delivered in the form of a gigantic two-million-euro commission. In about five pages, his letter went on to explain what had happened next and how, in the end, he had less money than before – which was, of course, all the fault of the cosmos. Or not? That was his question to me. While reading, I got the feeling the money had arrived too quickly. There are only few people who are spontaneously able to deal with lots of money in a sensible way. You read articles all the time about people who have won the lottery or inherited large amounts of money, and then lost everything again within a short time and ended up with less than they'd had before, maybe even having to take on extra debt. Just like this businessman, they didn't have time to learn how to manage such large funds wisely, and this sealed their fates. They hadn't had time to change their habits of inner thinking about money. A lack of money often goes hand in hand with fear and mental patterns of shortcomings and poverty. If you want to be rich, you should make your inner peace with the subject of 'money' first. In a lot of cases, it's this that's missing.

Pay attention to your own feelings when receiving money. Which statement represents your feeling best?

- 'Oh how nice, there's some wonderful money coming to me again. I am grateful for everything that comes to me and am sure that I will make sensible use of it.'

Or:

- 'I always get so little. That won't last very long either. Poor me!'

What do you tend to think when spending money?

- 'Nice to have the opportunity to spend money on this. I am positive that I'll always have the money I need. I shall always spend money wisely and with love.'

Or:

- 'That's way too expensive! Oh my goodness, how am I supposed to cope given the little I have! I can already see it trickling away.'

The problem is that our subconscious subsists on habits. In such cases, this is what it will remember: 'Every time I have to deal with money, it triggers bad feelings within me.' The subconscious then associates 'a lot of money' with 'a lot of bad feelings' and that 'money is dangerous' and so tries to get rid of it – to spare us the bad feelings.

Unless you've made your inner peace with the subject of 'money', there will always be an invisible force pushing you to cast off the money you've received out of the blue as quickly as possible. To my mind, that's precisely what happened with the businessman. What he needs, in my view, is a slow and constant increase in revenue, on the one hand, and time, on the other, to be able to listen to himself and his inner voice and to form new thinking habits, such as, 'I like money, and I trust my money. It depends on what I do with it. Money itself is neither good nor bad; I'm the one pulling the strings…' or something along those lines. In the end, the easy money got him into more trouble than the debt he'd had before.

Fortunately, there's now another option. He studies this book on loving yourself with fervour and establishes a deep, stable contact with the core of his inner being. Next time the big money comes along it will also come easily. He won't lose touch with himself again and takes completely different decisions. Receiving millions of euros quickly is only a blessing if you're ready for it mentally.

I recently read that Robbie Williams was selling the multimillion-pound villa he'd bought only a year earlier.

I mentioned it to a friend, who said you read that kind of thing about celebrities all the time. I often get the feeling about money that if people acquire it too quickly, it leaves them emotionally confused. I have nothing against abundance, but you need to make sure your inner wealth grows at an equal pace (this is the reason why I wrote a book for wealthy people some time ago, a *Shopping Guide for Inner Wealth*. I thought the more affluent people, in particular, boost their inner wealth, the better for the rest of the world it will be.)

Love orders take time

When it comes to love affairs, prompt delivery isn't necessarily a godsend either. To illustrate this, let's take the example of the 20-year-old daughter of a friend of mine. She'd had a steady boyfriend for five years, who used to be her classmate back in school. When it was over, she had to have a new boyfriend 'right away'. She wanted to fall deeply in love again, and enjoy life. No problem, the passionate love arrived and the chemistry was right from the start. It sparked and sparked, and glowed and glowed, then only a few wisps of smoke remained and with a last little puff it was all over – after three weeks. Her mother knew that her child had known her first boyfriend inside out, with all his merits and flaws. She asked carefully what the new one was like. And soon it became obvious that the two had only known each other rather superficially. There was no basis for love to grow. Love emerges when you know the other person's every gesture and expression in their eyes, and know exactly what's going on in the depths of their soul; when you recognize precisely whether the other's reaction is shaped by their fear patterns, or fully by love. Until you know that, you know nothing, and your relationship is bound only to scratch the surface and will soon become boring.

You should therefore double-check the exact wording of your cosmic order or wish. Do you want to fall in love on the spot and hurl yourself into a relationship? Someone once said to me there's no expression with 'fall' that meant anything really positive, not even if the expression is 'to fall in love'. Falling in love is nice, but it only gets really good once you skip the 'fall in' and real love begins. Maybe the actual wish reads like this: I want a relationship that is characterized by true love. I don't mind if love takes time to grow, and to become deeper and stronger. Whether it arrives sooner or later, I'm open to everything.

Real love grows stronger over time

I know, this is rich, coming from me! Manfred and I had barely known each other for more than four hours when we started to discuss whether he should move into my place, or I into his. It was just crystal clear. But moving in together after a short time also caused a few problems. We

'Every step of life shows much caution is required.'

JOHANN WOLFGANG VON GOETHE

only started to get to know each other fully once already living together. That's not always a piece of cake. We used to have quite a few clashes at the beginning. I sometimes thought that some things might have been easier had we taken a bit more time to get to know each other properly first. More than ten years later, our relationship is much more wonderful than in the beginning, now that we actually know each other. As for me, I don't get as easily offended as I used to, but see and feel what's really going on inside him, knowing him much better now. I also understand today that many things I used to think were directed against me actually have absolutely nothing to do with me at all. This knowledge helps me to distance myself lovingly, if something comes up.

Listen to your heart's desires

Here's what's really important: what is it your heart actually desires? There's a curse in Chinese culture that's supposed to bring the other person bad luck: 'May all your wishes come true!' This curse relies on the knowledge that people often feel unhappy once there's nothing left to wish or strive for. It's also based on the fact that most people find it quite hard or even impossible to distinguish between their heart's and their head's desires. Dealing with all your heart's desires coming true is not a problem, but having all your head's desires fulfilled could really drag you into feeling deeply unhappy.

You can observe this even in children: if they find all their wishes immediately catered for, if they get to play with every toy they like, to eat whatever they want, to do any activity they fancy, they'll just feel more and more dissatisfied instead of feeling pleased. If we only fulfilled their true heart's desires (such as the wish for love, respect and a sense of security) and just a few selected head desires every now and then, they'd feel much happier. So in fulfilling all of their head's desires, instead of them having 'all they can desire', what they actually get is 'unhappiness because there are no more desires left'. Children are also the best example when it comes to living in the here and now and being happy, regardless of how many wishes on your list have been fulfilled or not. If we manage to take a childlike, unbiased and playful approach to life, we'll be much more likely to be happy – even if the 'Chinese curse' hits you and all your wishes come true immediately.

Exercise

Every now and again, do something without pursuing a proper purpose or target, maybe something that doesn't seem to make any sense at all. Something like sorting pebbles on the shore of a lake, watching leaves blowing on the wind, or inventing your very own symbol of luck, then taking a stick and drawing it onto the forest soil. Let your soul roam free and enjoy it. Feel into yourself while doing this. The better you are at it, the easier you'll be able to handle a quick fulfilment of your wishes – and the sooner your heart's desires will come true as well by the way, as your intuition will be invariably more powerful as your skills in feeling and perceiving the smallest nuances grow stronger.

The Miracle of Loving Yourself

If you manage to behave in a childlike way as an adult, you can experience many miracles. The child within you will love you for every single game you play, oblivious to time and paying no heed to performance. Your soul can take a deep breath if you do, and love you for it. So will your immune system, your body and your heart if you're completely with yourself, like a child, and everything else becomes insignificant. Then they can truly unwind and relax. Your heart and inner perception open up. All of a sudden you see a miracle in everything around you.

Loving Body, Mind and Spirit

♥♥♥♥

I recently talked to a psychologically oriented homeopathic practitioner who said she practically does nothing other than teach people to love themselves. Loving yourself, she went on, is all that really matters, regardless of what area you are currently dealing with. The better you manage to love yourself, the sooner you will recover. While trying to achieve this, you can specifically activate and intensify your self-love on the physical, mental and emotional level. Let's take a more detailed look at the individual areas, so I can show you a few effective exercises.

Do you love your body?

How does it sound, when you look in a mirror and say to yourself: 'Dear body, I love you!' Do you believe what you are saying, or does it sound flat and phoney? Now, be honest! 'Well, I don't look that bad, really. Okay, I love myself to some extent…' When you said that, did you spend the last three hours getting ready first and face your mirror in the prettiest outfit your wardrobe had to offer? Is that true, genuine, and unconditional love? This morning, unfortunately while I was taking a shower, I suddenly realized I hadn't yet said anything nice to myself. Well, no problem, I'll just make up for it straight away. With this honourable intention in mind I stepped out of the shower – still wearing my granny's good old shower cap – and looked in the mirror. Honestly, I literally jumped back in shock seeing myself like that, and the smile on my face faded away. 'So, what was the deal with loving myself unconditionally again?' I wondered, and carefully peeked around the corner to face the mirror once again. After a number of attempts and a great deal of coaxing, I managed to face my reflection and was even able to find a suitable sentence: 'Even if I happen to be the ugliest person in the world, I love and accept myself the way I am', I declared, putting on a friendly smile for myself. This, together with the shower cap, presented such a sorry sight that I just couldn't help but burst out laughing: 'Don't worry, my darling, I like myself, no matter how silly I look right now.' In that moment, a proper wave of joy and relief rushed through me, which I expressed in the following sentence: 'I love myself simply because I'm here, because I'm alive.' The whole scenario was actually just a little game I played with myself. Still,

I had the impression that my subconscious was actually heart-stricken when I jumped back in shock at the sight of myself. However, it is equally as happy and relieved when I love myself regardless of how I look.

Now I have told you this short anecdote, I'll show you a couple of exercises that can help you to activate your self-love on the physical level.

Exercise

- In your mind, breathe in to and out of all areas of your body consecutively. While doing so, imagine breathing in love and gratitude, and breathing out old, unfriendly thoughts about yourself and the flaws you appear to have.
- Loving your body means getting exercise in the fresh air. Begin by taking at least ten-minute walks every day. Important: don't get upset because it eats away at your time; take your body for a walk, filled with love and gratitude. 'Dear body, I'm grateful to you and give you time, fresh air and love.' Breathe fresh air and love into all areas of your body in turn. 'Thank you, my dear body, for being there for me, I love you.'
- Mentally stroke your body from the inside. From within yourself, send love and gratitude to all your

body cells. Imagine you had hands that stroke everything from within you, from the feet up to your head. Mental stroking is now experiencing a huge increase in popularity. The first time I heard of it was when my Tai Chi teacher told me about it more than 15 years ago. In the last few years I've encountered it more and more frequently, once when I was talking to an African, and most recently a Russian doctor. Apparently, people are stroking themselves from within all over the world. And they all swear by the incredible power of this exercise. Don't just take my word for it; try it to see how your own body reacts to it, for yourself.

- Of course, stroking from the outside is a great exercise, too – gently stroke all the areas of your body you can reach.

Do you love your mind?

Your mind looks forward to affectionate attention as well. You can give it what it needs by feeding it – uplifting and encouraging it with positive information and ideas, as well as constructive conversations. Particularly in the mornings and evenings make sure to add positively stimulating ideas. This is equally important for both mental and physical food. Eating heavily in the morning and evening is a tough task for your digestive system to deal with. In the morning,

‘If thou wilt make a man happy, add not unto his riches but take away from his desires.’

Epicurus

the body is still detoxifying and in the evening the digestive system is already starting to slow down (and a late meal ends up sitting around overnight and starts fermenting). If you want to take in anything that could be hard to digest for your body and mind, you should ideally do so in the middle of the day. Otherwise, go for Shakespeare and wish-fulfilment coaching rather than thrillers and world news (even those can begin to ferment in your subconscious quite a bit overnight).

Exercise

'Become the light you yourself wish to see in the world!' This is an example of an easily digestible affirmation for the early morning.

If you do a relaxation exercise before going to sleep, you'll sleep more soundly and restfully. You can also use CDs with music and guided relaxation exercises to achieve this.

Or you can guide yourself. For example, you can go back through your day again, and mull over all the good things that happened and for which you are grateful. You can be grateful for pretty much everything: the sun, the air, and the bed you sleep in. Gratitude releases a vibration that evokes more and more reasons to be thankful. That's why this exercise is always well worth doing.

It doesn't matter which exercise of this kind you choose to do, you'll soon feel fitter than if you go to sleep with the usual stress in your system.

Do you love your soul?

Imagine you had a time machine and could travel back in time and meet your past self. Would two kindred souls be facing each other (and they really couldn't be any more kindred, could they?), two spirits who sense each other's heartbeat and feel happily united? Or would this someone (your past self) view you in a rather reserved and judgemental way? If you truly love the core of your inner self, your soul, it's absolutely obvious you would be more than delighted to meet yourself and that there would be friendly communication between the two of you. If, however, you would act rather coolly, then it's just as clear how little love there is in your soul for yourself and the core of your inner self.

Exercise

Go to the bathroom and greet your second self in the mirror. Look yourself deep in the eyes, into the depths of your soul, and greet yourself lovingly – and the more ardent the better. Being cool is completely inappropriate when practising your self-love skills.

While looking yourself in the eyes, you obviously shouldn't just be trying to establish their precise colour. Just imagine, there is a new person standing in front of you, and you are trying to work out this person's character, judging from the expression in their eyes. Let your eyes in front of the mirror take on an expression that will say to the other eyes in the mirror: 'Hello, it's really nice to meet you. Let me give you a warm and heartfelt welcome.'

Everything that feeds your soul also consolidates your love for yourself, especially when you do it in full awareness of your love for yourself. Put together a list of soul food and include everything you can think of: reading poems, being out in nature, taking a hot bath, enjoying your favourite tea while listening to your favourite music, dancing to your favourite music, completely oblivious to the world around you, or whatever you like.

Or perhaps this example will appeal to you. Go into the woods and look at the trees. None is perfect. Each one is somehow curved, crooked, gnarled and differently flawed. Choose one that seems to be kind of similar to you. Give it a hug and love it for what it is. Love yourself as well for who you are and imagine the tree is giving you its love back in return. It's such a great exercise; you've just got to try it! Off to the woods with you…

The Miracle of Loving Yourself

If you look after your body, mind and spirit lovingly, you will be rewarded with a bumper harvest. You'll feel better in your body, mind and spirit and the connection to your intuition will grow stronger, because you'll be much more sensitized to hearing the little and larger messages from within yourself. Here's a typical example. You'd like to get up and do something, when suddenly a thought springs to mind: 'Call person XYZ first.' You follow the spontaneous impulse and it turns out that the person you called has just thought of you as well and was just about to call you. Such little miracles become more frequent the closer you become to your inner self, and the more in harmony you are with yourself.

Part 3

On the Path… to Becoming a Self-love Professional

Forgiveness Becomes Easier

When your love for yourself grows, your heart will open to the world. It's when we begin to truly recognize ourselves and others, and to develop empathy. And this is why we denigrate and blame both ourselves and others less. We sense when we are causing ourselves and others pain, we begin to forgive ourselves and others. Here I'd like to quote from a letter from a participant in one of my seminars:

'I am a department manager in a boutique and have a colleague who always acted very chummily towards me and swore that we were the best of friends. But she was rude about me behind my back to the owner of the shop and my other colleagues. In truth she didn't particularly like me, but as I was the department manager, she had to live with the situation and me. When I found out, I was so hurt that I wanted vengeance. I knew of two or three lies she had told about me and wanted to expose them in front of my colleagues as if by accident. I had planned to do this after I had taken this seminar.

'Then I came home from the seminar with the 'I love myself, whatever you all think of me' mantra. The more often I recited it to myself, the better I was able to feel it and the more my wish for vengeance dissipated. I even felt sympathy and it occurred to me how little my colleague must love herself when she believed she had to weave a tissue of lies just to be able to survive. I suddenly felt sorry for her and I couldn't and didn't want to avenge myself on her anymore. I distanced myself from this pseudo-friendship to preserve myself, and meanwhile have been able internally to let go of the whole business. Interestingly enough, shortly afterwards some of her lies became exposed all by themselves and the sales team are now sorting it out among themselves. I am not involved in the mess at all and have my peace and quiet. If I had instigated the exposure myself, I would have been at the centre of all the stress. Thank you for the love yourself mantra. I will always make use of it when arguments or disagreements threaten. I am already looking forward to the next change of perspective it will bring about.'

You can also try to forgive others through your love for yourself, using the following exercise.

Exercise

Is there someone who often annoys you, by whom you feel humiliated, sidelined, deceived, put in a bad light, or who tries to make you feel guilty? If this is the case, consider the annoying feeling and examine how uncomfortable it is for you on a scale of one to ten. Ten equals 'extremely unpleasant', one equals 'only bothers me a little'. Then, in your mind, begin softly and lovingly to say to yourself: 'I love myself, regardless of whether anybody else does. I will always stay true to myself, no matter what happens around me. I love myself exactly the way I am. Even if I don't like everything I do, I always love myself in spite of everything, and with everything that I am. Mistakes and weaknesses are human, they are the quirks that make me who I am, and that is why I am worth loving along with them. I love myself in any case and will do so forever.' Take a deep breath into your belly and very slowly breathe out again (this is calming and makes room for more fresh oxygen when you breathe in again). Feel completely centred and love yourself.

Now think about the person from the beginning of the exercise. How unpleasant is the annoying feeling now on a scale of one to ten? Has anything changed?

The world around you mirrors the world within

So we can measure how much our self-love is growing by the fact that it becomes ever easier to forgive other people – their crankiness, their quirks and their meanness. Here the world around us is also a reflection of our inner world, as we have already seen with the subject of acceptance.

Whenever we blame other people it only really shows that we still feel guilt within ourselves. For example, a woman finds that her husband is constantly being unfriendly towards her and therefore it is his fault that she is unhappy. In truth, she is only expressing her general unhappiness through many little pokes and veiled criticisms that annoy him and make him act in an unfriendly manner. She doesn't make this connection, but rather only sees fault within her husband.

In this way, we always project our feelings of guilt onto our surroundings, and by doing so weaken ourselves. If we were to forgive ourselves and others, our self-love would grow and make us stronger.

So forgiveness is an important building block on the path to loving ourselves. You could also paraphrase forgiveness as 'overcoming rejection'. When I practise forgiveness, I accept what I was previously rejecting, just the way it is. And – here's a little trick – I accept myself, every part of myself. You can delve deeper using the following exercise.

Exercise

In this exercise we practise a little ritual. First, make a firm connection to your heart. The best thing to do is to put both your hands over your heart and feel the warmth of your hand on your breast. Then, very consciously breathe in and out and feel how your hands rise and fall on your breast. Now turn your thoughts to the subject of 'blame'. What emotions does it stir within you? What feeling wants to show itself? Do you feel anger welling up within you against a certain person? Do you feel anger against yourself because maybe you feel that you have done something wrong? Or are you struggling internally against fate itself, which you wish to blame for misfortunes that have occurred in your life? Whatever you find, with this ritual the easiest method is to work through all the possible ways of forgiveness one by one. You can forgive in six different ways:

- 'I forgive myself for the blame that I know of and recognize.'
- 'I forgive myself for the blame that I am subconscious of and which slumbers within me.'
- 'I forgive others for the blame that I consciously lay at their doors.'
- 'I forgive others for the blame that I subconsciously lay at their doors.'
- 'I also forgive the highest power (the cosmos or God) for the blame that I consciously lay on them (such as for the problems in my life).'
- 'I also forgive the highest power (the cosmos or God) for the blame that I subconsciously lay on them.'

You can find your own choice of words when doing this exercise. It is the intention that counts. The stronger the connection between you and your heart, the more successfully you will be able to forgive in the sense of 'I forgive myself for my stubbornness. I would like to forgive my stubbornness, here and now, from the bottom of my heart. I also forgive myself for everything I subconsciously blame myself for.'

Or: 'I forgive XYZ for speaking ill of me. I would like to forgive XYZ, here and now, from the bottom of my heart. I forgive every single person for the things that I subconsciously blame them for. And I forgive fate or the cosmos for the things I consciously or subconsciously blame them for. I would like to forgive them here and now, from the bottom of my heart.'

The Miracle of Loving Yourself

Loving yourself always goes hand in hand with opening your heart. When your heart opens, love for yourself will grow in parallel. And this love will then show itself in all of the facets that love can have, like a colourful bunch of flowers: sympathy, acceptance, forgiveness, fulfilment. When you love yourself, words that previously sounded like an offence now simply sound like a different opinion.

‘The weak can never forgive. Forgiveness is the attribute of the strong.’

Mahatma Gandhi

The Sound of Loving Yourself

♥♥♥♥

Whether people enjoy music isn't merely a question of the musician hitting the right note, but rather of how he hits that note; that is, what emotion he hits it with. If he simply rattles off a tune so that it is technically perfect, but gives it no heart, the audience won't jump up from their seats to applaud. A different singer might not always hit the right notes but puts his heart into his performance, and the result might be that the audience explodes in appreciation. Not only is the melody transported, but also the emotions resonate. This not only applies to music, but also to every type of communication. It means that we always completely out ourselves on the level of our subconscious communication. The subconscious of the person opposite will therefore always know whether I love myself or not – it can tell from the sound of my voice.

We can also observe this effect in ourselves. When we don't feel comfortable in the company of certain people, or we are under pressure, we no longer speak in our normal voice, as we alter our tone. This is an interesting phenomenon. For example, we pitch our tone just a little deeper than it is naturally so that no one can hear our nervousness, stress or emotional pain and in this artificial tone of voice we can control ourselves to such an extent that we sound 'even and emotionless' or 'relaxed'.

I myself get the impression that I nearly always use my 'own' voice when I give lectures, but almost never do so in conflict situations with individual people – and also not with people who generally stress me or I find strenuous. Once I caught myself using this kind of unnatural tone and tried to find the pitch of my natural voice. But even after several attempts, my pitch was still too high. The person opposite me looked concerned and went to fetch me a glass of water because he thought I had a frog in my throat. How embarrassing!

Then I turned to the following mantra (of course, only in my mind!): 'I love myself and allow myself to be loved. Whatever you think of me will have no influence over how much I love myself or the permission to be loved.' A few minutes later my natural tone of voice had returned completely by itself and a couple of minutes after that the voice of the person I was having the conversation with also changed. All of a sudden he sounded much nicer and more relaxed. Clearly he had experienced the same kind of stress with me as I'd had with him, and we had both distorted our voices.

Sounding natural

When we distort our voices, we are trying to be a different person to the one we really are. We take cover behind sounds to disguise who we actually are from other people. This is a real shame, as our natural pitch is the sound of relaxed self-love and...

- It is infectious and creates a natural atmosphere.
- It strengthens the connection to others.
- It raises your feeling of comfort.
- It relaxes you and your conversation partner.
- It even strengthens your immune system, according to my healer.
- And brings about a state of deep relaxation, which improves your access to your intuition. (If you often speak in a voice that is foreign to yourself and your subconscious, then you become a stranger to yourself and your intuition).

You will feel better with the sound of self-love in your voice, you will find it easier to be authentic and you will hear the voice of your intuition more clearly. This natural sound is automatically stable, when your self-love is also stable. But, on the other hand, you can also strengthen your love for yourself by consciously observing and applying the sound of your natural voice. This is similar to breathing: when you are relaxed, you automatically breathe calmly. If, however, you get stressed, you can reduce your stress and return to a relaxed state by consciously controlling your breathing.

Tip

If you are someone who speaks a great deal and often uses a 'self-protecting tone of voice', then the easiest way for you to recover your natural tone of voice is by speaking to little children or animals. Even a ladybird will work. The important thing is that it is an animal or insect that you like and seems harmless to you.

If, on the other hand, you want to know how you sound when using an unnatural tone of voice, you could go to the zoo and crouch down at a window in front of a bored tiger. Then try to get the animal to respond to you with a warm gesture by speaking to it. You will be able to hear all sorts of strange tones coming out of your mouth – while all of the other visitors to the zoo will be asking themselves if you are feeling quite well. And if you then notice that you are speaking to your boss in the same tone that you used with the tiger, then just imagine during your next conversation that he is a sweet little ladybird and would love you to set him on a leaf. You are sure to feel more relaxed then and your boss will be happier to listen to what you say.

Exercise

Observe the way you speak and the pitch of your voice when talking to friends, relatives, children, colleagues, people you love or dislike, people who are very close to you or others who are complete strangers. Discover your very own natural tone of voice and apply it consciously, to create a natural atmosphere. If it doesn't work, repeat the following mantra in your mind, 'I love myself and allow myself to be loved' and see whether it becomes easier for you over time to use your natural tone of voice. Create your own little 'I love myself' mantra. Choose a form of words that you enjoy and which kindles a childlike happiness within you. The sentence can be very sensible, crazy or wild; whatever suits you best. Don't worry about whether the song would make a good impression on others, or whether it is professional – the only thing that counts is that you find pleasure in it. Here are three examples:

♥ ♥ ♥ ♥

'I love myself and I love you. Love is wonderful and so are you.'

♥ ♥ ♥ ♥

'Everything about me is great, I am my very best mate. I am allowed to love me and be completely free.'

♥ ♥ ♥ ♥

'With heartfelt courage and power, my life is a beautiful arbour. I love me and I love you, life without love can never be true.'

♥ ♥ ♥ ♥

Find words that are as personal and individual to you as you can. Find a sentence that really fits and touches you. Then simply start singing, creating your own melody. As we already know, neither the tempo nor the notes have to be perfect in order to positively influence you and your subconscious. Invent a dance to go with your tune, wild and strange or slow and stately, dance just the way you are, and only for yourself. And the important part of the exercise is to let your voice sound just the way it sounds when everything in your life is perfect. Move your body in the way you do when you are happy, relaxed and serene. Many of the participants at our seminars have already discovered that a few minutes of dancing around wildly and singing ensure that you are in a good mood for hours – provided that you can overcome your inhibitions.

When the beast within you growls

Sometimes the beast hiding inside each one of us puts a brake on our good mood and ensures that we don't feel as free and as motivated as we could to sing and dance. Are you still sending out vibrations of doubt through your voice and movements? Then it is high time to have a serious word: 'Dear beast, it is okay that you exist and that you also want to have a say sometimes. But it must also be possible that you shut your trap and disappear for at least five minutes – and I mean properly and right now! Go on, get lost, now, off you go!'

Then channel all of your energy into your voice and movements, until you feel completely free. You might have to be pretty wild at first, until your beast has actually disappeared completely. But even if you only manage to keep it up for three minutes, it will have an immense effect on your subconscious. It will probably wake up feeling totally baffled and say: 'Hello, hello, hello, have I missed anything? Have we won the lottery, or what? All right, don't worry, I'm here. I will turn all the dials in our body chemistry, our hormones and immune system to the happy, happy and yet happier setting. Oh, and another thing, hey intuition, can you come out of your shell again? There's a party going on here. You can get busy straight away in looking for great opportunities for yet more happiness and self-love, yippee!'

When your beast has finally disappeared, it usually won't reappear all that quickly. And should it turn up again and start to annoy you, just try another little dancing session. The most important thing is that it takes a break from all its doubting, so that your voice can ring out loud and clear, filled with power and happiness. The more often you apply the sound and movements of self-love, the deeper you anchor your love for yourself within you and the more it will grow.

The Miracle of Loving Yourself

A saying by the Indian Dr Madan Kataria is often quoted in laugh yoga clubs: 'We don't laugh because we are happy, we are happy because we laugh.' An acquaintance of mine who is a psychiatrist carried out tests on people suffering from heavy depression and asked them to raise the corners of their mouths as high as they could for five minutes each day. She was then able to reduce the amount of anti-depressant drugs they were taking straight away by 50 per cent. This sounds like a miracle. You can discover your own miracle of growing happiness in life by inducing regular periods of happiness for no apparent reason.

Be Stable in Your Energy

♥♥♥♥

I recently read an article in which an English healer reported that he had met only three people in the past ten years who spent more than 30 per cent of their time in their own energy fields. In order to avoid pain, injury, loss and disappointment, most people absorb the energy that their parents, partners, colleagues, neighbours, people in authority and others are sending out, and put their own energy on the back burner. This statement shocked me. Even though it isn't that surprising, because there is so much tumult on earth and every person uses another person as their focal point, rather than their own truth. And, after all, those whom others take as their point of orientation are equally unstable in their own field of energy. In fact, they in turn orientate themselves on other unstable people.

If what the healer said is anywhere near the truth, this would mean that armies of unstable people are orientating themselves on armies of other unstable people, who are doing the exact same thing themselves. Each person hopes that the other knows more, that they are more stable and secure than they are themself – never guessing that that person only crows so loudly so that no one notices that they are just as unstable as the rest of us. This reminds me of a girl I know. She is about to do her GCSE exams and doesn't know yet what to do afterwards.

Her mother is pushing her to do one thing, her father to do another and her teacher is busy cajoling her to take another path he thinks is absolutely the best way for her to go. I sent the child to an acquaintance of mine for careers advice. She called me up and said that she couldn't really do much for the girl. She was such a stranger to herself that one would probably need to spend a whole year working with her until she was back in tune with herself enough to be able to answer the decisive questions. 'What can I do, what do I want to do, what do I believe I am capable of, and what do I enjoy?' The girl was only in the habit of asking herself one question: 'In what ways do I have to contort myself, so that everyone else finds me okay?' But at that moment, three very different people wanted to pull her in three different directions, and no matter which way she decided to go, she would upset two of them. This prospect really scared her – and asking her to tune in to her own feelings was impossible. Fundamental work in 'loving herself' was necessary first.

Listening to yourself

This brings us back to the subject, as being stable within you means:

- Loving yourself.
- Honouring yourself.
- Respecting yourself with all your peculiarities and idiosyncrasies.
- Supporting yourself in fulfilling yourself.
- Having access to your own truth at all times.
- Being able to embrace your own truth without fear.
- Treating the tugging and pushing of others with understanding and sympathy, without losing sight of your own truth.
- Being able to feel yourself and your motivation and question it each and every moment – without ever losing your love for yourself.

Let's assume that you catch yourself falling into a typical, age-old, self-obstructing trap, a pattern of behaviour that is damaging to you. You can make it all much worse by blaming yourself, 'Oh you idiot, how long are you going to continue behaving like such a fool?', but you can also think, 'Aha! So I have slipped back into this pattern of behaviour, this unhelpful habit, now that's interesting. But of course this won't prevent me from loving myself for an instant in any shape or form. Let's see, what would I like to do in this situation? What is the best way for me to return to the flow? What is the right thing to do to make me feel rounded, whole and healthy again?'

You will become more stable by establishing new, loving patterns in your behaviour towards yourself. And also through lots of little moments in which you accept and honour yourself, no matter what you have just observed yourself doing again. Always try to work with yourself in a playful way!

No distractions

Talking of being playful, I recently made an agreement with myself that I really wanted to meditate one evening, but when the time came I really didn't feel like it. I actually felt like watching a romantic comedy on DVD instead. So I asked my inner wisdom whether it'd be possible to watch the film in such a way that it was similar to meditating. And then I had an idea how to do it. I decided, while watching, to examine every single little emotion that germinated inside me very precisely, feel my way deep inside it and take the opportunity to bring hidden motivations and suppressed feelings up and expose them to the light of day. I decided that I would press the pause button each time and first delve into the feeling deeply before I continued watching.

It was a great idea and I started straight away – and it took about an hour just to get through the first five minutes of the film. I had barely watched the intro and had already examined 'fear of other people's negative emotions', 'fear of shame and ignominy', to name but two. This was too much psychology for the evening – too much hard work. So I decided to meditate after all. And the question briefly occurred to me of whether it is possible that I was being taken for a ride by my higher self, and if there were another part of me sitting somewhere and having a good laugh at my expense… But the thought melted away and I got on with my silent meditation.

So you see, you don't have to turn your whole life on its head to be able to develop more love for yourself. Whatever you do, however mundane the task, you always have the following choice: you can either distract yourself from yourself and continue to absorb the energy of those around you until the end of time, which you then take as being truer than your own truth, or you can start to recognize and honour yourself, delve deeply into your emotions – no matter where you might be at the time and what you might be doing.

Love attracts love

One day, after extensive exercises in loving myself (the ones in the next chapter), I took the train into the city. It was, as always, very busy. Usually the people take a seat in the train with a huffy, unwelcoming expression on their faces and look away quickly if you try to flash a friendly smile at them or, heaven forbid, even say 'hello'. But on this day, every person who took a seat next to me smiled and greeted me politely. I had to change trains and it happened in both of them. I spoke about it later to a small meditation group I belong to and everyone had experienced the same phenomenon. Love attracts love. The huffy grumpy people take a seat somewhere else when you are radiating love. The way it works is really very simple:

- The more self-love and self-respect you have, and the more stable it is, the more loving people and situations you will attract.
- The more love you have, the more you are able to give. You can either infect other people, or you stay emotionally stable and are at peace within yourself, even when others act in an unfriendly way towards you.
- You become ever more stable, the more often you listen in to yourself and treat yourself in a loving way – whatever you discover. Ask yourself: 'Let's see, what would I like to do in this situation? What is the quickest way to return to the energetic and emotional flow? What is the right thing to do to achieve a healthy holistic state of being?'

'To love oneself is the beginning of a lifelong romance.'

Oscar Wilde

- Love yourself, regardless of whether you have just caught yourself having good or bad thoughts.
- Honour your individuality, respect yourself and train yourself in new habits.

Exercise

Whenever you get the feeling that you are on the verge of allowing yourself to be knocked off balance by someone else's truth, pause for a moment and speak silently to yourself. Find a form of words that works for you. Here are a few examples:

- Even if you don't like me, I love myself, just the way I am.
- Even if you are convinced that I am doing everything wrong, or it seems as if I am, I love myself. I permit myself to follow my own path.
- I am responsible first and foremost to the truth of my own heart.
- I hope that you will always be able to follow the truth of your own heart. And I hope that it will also be good for you as I follow the truth of my heart, even if it is not the same as yours. If you feel bad about this, I feel for you, I am sorry for you, but I am important to myself. I am living my own truth, not yours.

You can also review the day in your mind at night before you fall asleep, and consider whether you are content with yourself. How well did you manage to feel yourself, stand by yourself and live your truth? If you didn't manage to consider what your truth would be in a couple of situations because it was all so hectic, take the time now. Feel inside yourself and find out. You might like to let a little film play out in your mind's eye in which you act in the way you would have liked.

The more often you take time for yourself, the more stable and at peace you will become within yourself, and the more time you will spend in your own field of energy. And you will make an amazing discovery: all the other people for whose sake you used to contort yourself very often won't be upset at all, but rather feel incredibly attracted to your new power and the love you radiate. Take time to discover and listen to your very own personal truth.

The Miracle of Loving Yourself

Even an emotionally unstable person who doesn't like to take decisions, whose opinion sometimes turns like a weather vane in the wind, who is easily confused and tired, can become a stable emotional pillar of strength. Such stability grows out of the truth within your heart, out of love and respect for yourself. In this way, you will be able to ensure that you are always taking the right decision, especially if you don't allow yourself to be swayed by people who always create a lot of pressure and noise about everything. Stand by yourself. Take time to question your heart, to discover your own truth. Then the miracle can occur, and out of a weather vane buffeted by the wind, a calm, centred, pillar of strength can arise instead.

Are You Good at Being Alone?

♥♥♥♥

I have just read in the newspaper about a very young starlet who takes lots of different drugs, can't spend a minute alone, always drags a train of people around with her and flits from one party to the next. Apparently she also wants to commit suicide, because she has to go to prison for 30 days. She can't handle even the idea of spending all that time completely alone, without parties or alcohol.

I also enjoy living in freedom, but 30 days of peace away from everything, with meditation, yoga… well, I don't think it would be that bad. At any rate, I wouldn't have a reason to kill myself. But I tried to imagine what it'd be like to be in the starlet's shoes. What would I be feeling?

On film I would always be the heroine, but secretly I would think: 'I am not really as wonderful and flawless as the heroines I play. People mistake me for the heroine.

But actually I am a failure, I am not as strong as the girl on screen…' I would have absolutely zero love for myself and would therefore not be able to stand myself. I wouldn't be able to love myself because I couldn't measure up to the image the general public have of me. I would feel like a failure, the biggest loser of all time – but nobody would be allowed to find out. That's why I would always need to be surrounded by my 'tumult of stardom', because then I wouldn't have to face up to my fear of failure. I'd really want to be like the heroines I play. But then there would be a part of me that would struggle against this, because I would then be thinking, 'It's only acting after all, it's not the real me.' So I would tie myself up in knots trying to be different.

It would be a blessing for the starlet to love herself. Because then it would become completely irrelevant whether she really is like the characters she plays or not – it wouldn't matter. She could try out everything and wouldn't give two hoots about the opinions of others. The main thing is that what she does is good for her. The precondition for this though, is that she listens to her heart, which is something she hasn't had much practice at in her life so far. First she would need lots of time for herself.

You have to learn to be alone

Everyone is different. Some find it easy to spend time alone, while others don't. Some first have to explore and practise being alone; others have to learn social skills because they are alone too much. Spending time alone with yourself, of course, doesn't mean sitting at home and surfing the web. Spending time alone with yourself means really concentrating on who you are inside, without any distractions, and getting to know yourself better. After all, how are you going to love someone whom you hardly know? All love and every relationship gains depth and beauty the better one knows the other person. The same goes for loving yourself. So make sure that above everything else you get to know yourself really well, so that you can enjoy the love you have for yourself in its fullest intensity.

Exercise: For beginners in being alone

- Do you still find it difficult spending time alone? No problem. Lock yourself into your bathroom for three minutes, stand in front of the mirror and look into your eyes. Who are you? Can you discover the core of love within you? How does this love within you express itself?
- Then close your eyes and feel inside yourself. What are you feeling in this exact moment? Who are you and how are you?
- After this you can plunge back into the tumult of life.
- Repeat this exercise daily. Slowly raise the dose.

Exercise: For advanced students in being alone

It's not a problem for you to sit alone in a beer garden, even when several people give you the sympathetic 'awww, you must be single' look. You don't care one bit? They should mind their own business? Great, then you can get going straight away by taking lonely walks in the countryside and asking yourself the following questions: 'How do I feel in this place, by this tree, in this clearing? How do I feel standing by this lake, in the wind, or the rain?' Being in the countryside is a particularly good place to explore the feelings within you. And if you find a place you love to be, you can take a notebook there (if you like that kind of thing) and make notes on what you discover about yourself.

You can also create a cosy 'I enjoy myself' place and from time to time hang a 'please do not disturb' sign on the door, so that you'll be left alone.

Exercise: For professionals in being alone

Of course, there are also people who live alone and are alone more often than they actually want to be. They clearly manage to survive being alone somehow. In this case the question would be: 'Is the time you spend with yourself just quantity time, or also quality time? How do you make use of the time you spend alone? Do you make use of it at all? What do you do to strengthen your inner qualities and your love for yourself? (Thankfully this book can offer some exercises). Are you good to yourself?' Look at it like this: a person who lives alone has a great deal of time to grow into a crystal that radiates out into the world. Don't struggle against your situation; rather use the time to deepen your love for yourself, maybe also to write love letters to yourself. This is a lot more fun than sulking!

The Miracle of Loving Yourself

For people who love themselves, being alone – that is being al-one – means being one with all. They find a great deal of beauty and happiness in it. For people who love themselves, being lonely is like being an only seed, a seed in the colourful garden of creation. The time spent alone is a time for self-reflection and discovery: what do I want to sow next?

Making Peace with Your Parents is Essential

♥♥♥♥

'Right, if you actually knew my parents, you wouldn't expect me to make peace with them!' I've often had this or similar things said to me. And I do understand there are some really extreme cases. There is only one catch: in purely genetic terms, 100 per cent of you comes from your parents (half from your mother and half from your father). And you carry your energetic-intellectual-emotional inheritance within you, whether you want it or not. If you are not at peace with your parents, you are rejecting far too large a part of yourself. You can't simultaneously reject your parents and love yourself.

A couple came up to me at one of my events and told me about their problem. The wife had had stress with her father for ages and her husband hated his mother. The couple had been together for two years and had noticed that it seemed almost as if the husband were turning into someone just like her father and the wife into someone just like his mother. They said that this hadn't been the case at the beginning, and both were at their wits' end. I recommended they try the exercise set out below. They should both try to put themselves in his mother's shoes first and then later her father's, and imagine they had lived their lives. Finally, they should ask each other how it had felt for them. Apparently, both partners tried fervently to do this and later got back in contact with me. After doing the exercises they had more understanding for their parents and were happy that they hadn't had to live their lives and were able to forgive them more easily. The wife even made peace with her father. The husband still didn't want to see his mother but didn't bear a grudge against her anymore. And on that very day he stopped acting like her father and she stopped acting like his mother. The absence of peace in their hearts had pushed each of them into behaving in exactly the right way to annoy the other, so that their partner came to represent everything they disliked about the parent they didn't love.

Why does this happen? The soul is always striving towards peace and repeats the unresolved parent problem with the partner, to give it another chance of being resolved.

So, no matter what your parents do, they have to look after themselves. But we should make our peace with them, at least internally – and for completely egotistical reasons. The love for ourselves can only be pure and show us the path to a harmonious, happy life, when we are at peace with our forebears.

Exercise

Imagine you were in your parent's shoes and had lived their life. You can't actually do this, but you can imagine it in your mind's eye.

Then observe what feelings and thoughts come to you and say to yourself, 'I am sorry that things are not working out. I thank myself for examining my feelings and the insights I have gained. I love myself'. Very often this is a simple but effective way to transform your anger into empathy and understanding. You recognize that even your parents acted out of pressing needs of their own. Had they been happy, fulfilled people, full of love and love for themselves, things would have been very different. Now wish them happiness and fulfilment. Even if they are no longer alive, you can send your wishes to them across the divide as energy. Imagine their souls waking up wrapped in a mantle of pure love. To finish, wish all of your forebears, especially those who annoy and anger you, love, light and inner peace. Wish them release from all their internal pressures and prisons.

Tip

Find a connection in your heart to 'Father heaven' and 'Mother Earth' and feel yourself safe in the lap of the 'divine parents' of all creation. This helps you to transcend your current problems with your biological parents and create 'cosmic parents' for yourself, the best parents anyone can have. Meditate using the mantra: 'Mother Earth loves me', 'Father heaven (or creation, or life) loves me.'

The Miracle of Loving Yourself

If you see yourself as someone who has a heap of morally rotten ancestors in your family tree, a part of you will always feel weak. If, however, you make peace with them internally and only keep the positive inheritance of your forebears in your thoughts, regardless of whether they were able to live up to it or not, you will have an unbelievable amount of potential power at your fingertips in terms of energy. In your mind's eye, you'll see yourself as someone with a strong inheritance. If you are then also able to see yourself as a much-loved child of heaven and earth, your sense of self-esteem will grow enormously.

The Source of Power within You

We usually hold our seminars in a room that is 250m² and shaped like a pyramid. One evening after dinner we carried out a guided relaxation exercise with everyone. Most people were lying on mats and had covered themselves up with blankets. When we finished at 9pm, everyone left the room and we locked it. One participant, however, only woke up then. She had been lying in a corner under her blanket, had fallen asleep and hadn't noticed that everyone was leaving. And because there was a pile of cushions in her corner too, we hadn't noticed her either. She was very shocked when she realized that she'd been left behind and locked in. As she later told us, she spontaneously thought: 'How typical for this to happen to me. No one ever notices that I am here and I'm sure that no one is missing me either. That's just the way people always treat me...' Her self-esteem plummeted.

After a short time, however, she decided to look after herself. She sat down, closed her eyes and opened a connection to the source of power within her heart. For some people it is the subconscious that knows so much more than the rational mind; for her it was the source of divinity within her, and it seemed that this divine source of power was giving her advice: 'Why don't you take advantage of this unusual situation and the power of the empty room for meditation? Take a seat in the middle, create a comfortable place for yourself and drink in the energy of this pyramid room.' This is exactly what she did and she soon slipped into the 'best meditation of her life', as she told us later. Her low self-esteem vanished, she felt like an Egyptian queen who was able to use the power of a huge pyramid, for herself alone.

'When the source of power within you is awakened through the belief in your divine source, the love for yourself that you have been striving for and an unconditional harmony with the flow of life will automatically follow.' I discovered this sentence, which so perfectly reflects this situation, on the home page of the healer Ramona (www.rastoa.de). This is precisely what our participant experienced on that evening: she felt at one with the cosmos; full of self-respect and happiness, and in tune with the flow of all creation.

Only later did she remember that the doors to the terrace could be opened from inside the room, and she could just walk out. So she went out, feeling cheerful and relaxed, and let the people at the bar know so that they could lock the other door.

Exercise

I also found another interesting page on Ramona's website that contains a wonderful exercise, which I summarize here with her permission. Your subconscious interprets a lack of love for yourself as criticism against creation: God didn't do a good job when he created me. So the snake bites its own tail. When I – usually in secret and subconsciously – feel neglected by God, my level of self-esteem is low. And because my level of self-esteem is low, it can only mean that creation slipped up. And because God messed up, he doesn't like me. That means that I am worthless… and so it continues.

When you discover patterns of thought like this within you, then release them consciously and immediately, and thank creation (God, your inner cosmos) for your life: 'You did a great job, thank you for my life!'

Feel within yourself to find out what you experience when you repeat these thoughts several times. What does your heart feel when you thank creation for the gift of your life? Say to yourself: 'Creation loves me, always and forever, no matter what happens. Creation loves everything it has brought into being and it also loves me – boundlessly.'

How does this feel? What changes do you experience in your level of self-esteem when you understand that the entire cosmos loves you?

The Miracle of Loving Yourself

Loving yourself is equivalent to your belief in the value of all creation. Loving yourself is the same as saying to creation, 'You did a great job when you created me'. Try to internalize this attitude! This will immediately become your way of connecting with the divine core inside you and to your intuition, and will strengthen all the subconscious powers within you.

‘There are only two ways to live your life. One is as though nothing is a miracle. The other is as though everything is a miracle. I believe in the latter.’

ALBERT EINSTEIN

Send Love to the Divine Core within You!

♥♥♥♥

A further way of drilling down to the core of wisdom at your centre and making friends with it is by means of a 'reading meditation'. I have put one together, inspired by the neuroscientist Joe Dispenza (see page 76), which I would like to share with you here. You can increase your love through this meditation to such an extent that you move closer to your deep subconscious and your own higher self. If you transcend the bounds of your own body you can also deepen your love for your divine core. If you are a more sober type of person, you can use this reading meditation to help you build a deeper appreciation for the controlling intelligence within you. You can try it out and see what happens within you.

Exercise: Reading meditation

Find a comfortable and relaxed position to sit or lie down in, and initially inhale and exhale a few times in a relaxed way. You can, for example, breathe in with your eyes closed and mentally count to three and then count to five while exhaling. Once you have started to feel relaxed, open your eyes and read the first sentence or sentences. Always only read a small part. Then close your eyes again and consider what you have read. Feel carefully within yourself and examine your emotions when you now repeat the words you have read to yourself. Then, when you feel you are ready, open your eyes and read the next little piece. The disadvantage of such a reading meditation compared to a spoken CD is that you read it yourself and need to open your eyes. The advantage is that you can go through it in your very own rhythm and can feel every trace of emotion within you to its full extent.

It is also conducive if you address the power within you, while you are doing this, in a way that suits you. This is why I will only include a 'Dear *' here and you can add to the address:

- ...higher intelligence
- ...deep subconscious
- ...higher self

- ...God
- ...divine core
- ...Mother of all creation

The reading meditation then works as follows:

'I lie back and relax and feel how the surfaces of my body are in contact with the ground below me.

I monitor my breathing and how deeply I breathe.

I simply lie/sit there and breathe, until my breathing is very soft and relaxed. Now I breathe in to and out of my heart in my mind's eye, perhaps I can also feel my heart beating.

I come ever closer and deeper to myself.

I love myself and allow me, from the bottom of my heart, to love myself.

Now I am ready to make contact with the power within me: Dear * in me and all around me. I know that you are there!

I know that in each one of the 70 to 100 billion cells in my body, about 100,000 chemical reactions occur every second.

100,000 chemical reactions per second in each cell – and almost without a single mistake, proven by the fact that I am here and I am alive.

It is very similar everywhere else in nature: millions and billions of individual events take place each second.

I now turn to * within me and all around me, who manages to coordinate all of this.

What a gigantic piece of work I see, what an enormous miracle is creation.

I would not be able to gain an overview of all of these events, not even for a minute fraction of a second, with my rational mind.

My existence and my life prove that you, dear *, are larger and more powerful than my rational mind.

I feel you, dear *, within me, how you watch over and control everything that happens.

How great must be your love for life, dear *, that you can create such complex processes and coordinate and maintain them – as everything that occurs within my body each second must work in harmony.

I decide here and now that I will learn from you and will nurture my love for life until it grows just as large as yours.

I will allow the love within my heart to grow larger and larger, with the help of the power of my imagination. After a time it will encompass the whole of my body, fill my surroundings and radiate out into the entire world.

I feel myself connected to the whole world and I feel that the entirety of creation is infused with an ordering power of the highest intelligence, consciousness and love.

From now on, I am on personal terms with you, dear *, within me and surrounding me.

When I eat I invite you, dear *, to digest the food and make the best use of it. (Imagine it doing this while you're eating and it will be easier for this exercise to come to mind when you're really eating and to practise it again.)

When I work, I invite you, dear *, to inspire me, to give me the best ideas and to constantly remind me of the wonder of life, even if I am just standing at the photocopier – it too is a miracle, just as I am, the air, earth and life itself, each thing is a miracle.

When I go to bed, I invite you, dear *, to accompany me in my dreams and ensure that my rest gives me peace and strength.

When I meet other people, I open my heart and feel you there, dear *. So that you can always remind me that only 'love', or the 'cry for love' exists. With this understanding all encounters will unfold in the best way possible.

(Whatever that means, remember the chapter on 'saying no' on page 45, and accept it with love as well.)

I'm thinking of a very personal situation that, from this moment on, I can also enrich through my contact to *. (This could be anything: walks in the countryside, pleasant or unpleasant situations, whatever you like.)

Dear *, in me and enveloping me, I thank you and I will come and visit you again soon. May love, light and laughter accompany us on our path along our ever-deepening friendship. May every person on earth discover this contact to you for themself.

May peace and love reign on earth.'

♥ ♥ ♥ ♥

And whenever you have felt and enjoyed enough, stretch out with pleasure and you'll find yourself back in your wonderful, conscious and ever-watchful daily rational consciousness.

My healer always has a wealth of wisdom and interesting comparisons ready. He believes that the rational mind is like a nail in the wall and the subconscious, with its higher intelligence, is like the wall the nail is in.

But the wall doesn't stand alone either; it is part of the house (the world) and cannot be separated from it. As the nail, we do not feel connected to the house, but in truth we are all individual elements of a greater whole and not separate from anything.

The Miracle of Loving Yourself

Recite the reading meditation almost as if * were some 'other person', not yourself. This approach makes it easier to establish contact with this being, which in truth is part of you. But because the rational mind can't locate it, it feels separated from it. The more often you carry out this exercise and the more love and feeling you put into it, the more rapidly the miracle will occur and you will suddenly feel at one with this power – and your rational consciousness will be on pause. True love for yourself encompasses the higher intelligence and the consciousness of the entire cosmos, because it's all part of you, after all. When you love the entirety of your being, you automatically love the entire world as well. This isn't so easy, but you can always practise it, without any pressure and while having a lot of fun!

Love Your Neighbour by Loving Yourself

There is a type of self-love that is not genuine. It is expressed in a loud, hard, vain and egocentric way and just tramples over other people. In truth, there is a large void in your heart and not a trace of true love for yourself. This is demonstrated when a person is forced to cope with themself in the absence of any distraction. Very often, this will cause them to break down completely.

True love for yourself is also the precondition for loving others. But this love can also be artificial and annoy other people or even cause damage. I would like to tell you the story of a participant from a seminar as an example, who completely sacrificed herself for her drug-addict daughter. Her entire life revolved solely around her. Her body and her gestures only expressed tortured suffering and concern for her daughter. We sent her to a therapist friend of ours and advised her to start taking care of herself more from now on. In this condition she was constantly sending the message to her daughter that, 'You are responsible for the fact that I feel so awful, because you are not living the way I want my daughter to live'.

Children, however, are not responsible for the happiness of their parents and it is no wonder that they rebel in the widest variety of ways against this. This is also what the therapist said to her, but in a more drastic way.

He said that through her complete self-sacrifice she was forcing her daughter more firmly into the arms of her drug addiction. He went on to say that no person is able to bear it when another sacrifices themself completely for them. No wonder then that her daughter felt she had to anaesthetize herself all the time.

Do not forget yourself

What followed was a difficult and stony path for the mother. But she forced herself to start going out with friends again, to games evenings, to the theatre, for walks and other activities. In agreement with her therapist, she had told her daughter that she was no longer prepared to let her happiness in life depend on her. If her daughter really wanted to change something, such as through rehab, she would always be there to help her. Otherwise she would now start to enjoy her life again, no matter what her daughter decided to do.

The decisive breakthrough came while her mother was on a hiking trip and her daughter called her up on her mobile because she had lost her door key. She wanted her mother to come home and unlock the door for her. The mother's initial impulse was to drop everything and drive home immediately. But then she came to her senses and said, 'No, I'm sorry I can't. I am hiking with friends and won't be home until tomorrow. You'll have to find somewhere else to sleep. Call your grandmother, or Aunt Lotta, I am not cutting short my wonderful hiking holiday.' Her child screamed that she hated her stuffy aunt, that grandma would only start criticizing her, and there was no way she was going to call them… but this time her mother stayed calm, 'Well, that makes no difference then. You are always telling me how much you hate me. Why should I bend over backwards and let somebody who hates me spoil my weekend, even if it is my own daughter? I am sorry, but you'll have to find a solution yourself, I am not coming.'

Escaping the role of victim

From that day on, the mother began to feel ever more comfortable in her new life. The daughter, however, needed longer to get used to her new mother. She was bitterly angry that her mother was no longer at her beck and call as before – although she had absolutely despised her for being so. The daughter was forced to end her laziness and take more responsibility for herself. Her mother's attitude remained clear and firm. She continually reasserted that she loved her daughter and wished that she could find the right path to a happy life. She was also ready to help at any time that her daughter really needed her. But she would no longer sacrifice herself by driving to the ends of the world at night to pick her up and things like that. It had already been proven that it didn't really help anyway. 'Well, at least one of us is happy now, and that is me,' the mother realized.

It took another year until her daughter was free of the drugs. Another six months passed until she admitted that a great weight was lifted off her shoulders when she no longer felt responsible for her mother's happiness in life. Even if she had taken a while to come to this conclusion, in the end she felt a lot better since she had assumed responsibility for her own welfare and her mother no longer tried to take it away from her.

Of course this chain of events can't be applied to every case of drug addiction, but it does demonstrate very clearly the way in which love for others is much more effective if the level of love for yourself is sufficient.

- ♡ Through love for yourself you are much better able to gauge the true needs of the other person. Sometimes a single 'no' is far healthier that a string of 'yeses'.
- ♡ You are only able to give to others what you possess already. If you sacrifice yourself entirely for others, without watching out for yourself, this will drain you

until you are completely empty, and you will have nothing more to give.

- If you have learned to take responsibility for your inner happiness and not to burden others with this responsibility, you will also be able to teach others to do this and be a living example to them.
- When you are 'full up' inside, you will be glad to give to others. Giving from an inner profusion will make you feel happy and fulfilled. The other person will see that you are doing it gladly. On the other hand, if you are drained and exhausted and still give, the other person will feel guilty for being an additional burden to you.

Exercise

Whenever someone asks you to do something large, allow yourself some time to consider before you answer. Take calm and relaxed breaths into your belly and say to yourself in your mind: 'I love myself, I am pure love. I wish this person the very best.' Feel the love.

Then ask yourself: 'How can I help most effectively and what kind of help really makes sense now? What do I actually want to do?' You don't automatically have to do what the other person asks you to do. Perhaps the other person wants to borrow money, but you have the impression that they are very bad at dealing with money. Maybe you feel the need to help them search for a job, or whatever seems sensible.

Listen to your inner voice, and have the courage to say 'no', if you don't feel good about carrying out the request.

The Miracle of Loving Yourself

If I treat myself lovingly and respectfully and communicate this, then this behaviour will very quickly become second nature to me. After all, we spend most of our time with ourselves. If I go through life calmly, trusting that I am worthy of love and am loved by God and by life, just the way I am, then this will also become a fundamental tenet of my life. Soon other people will also appear much more loveable to me. When I am able to love myself, with all of my faults and weaknesses, I will be more capable of smiling wryly over faults and weaknesses in others. Loving myself automatically leads me to view the world in a loving way. The best we can do for others is to begin by loving ourselves.

Obituary

By Manfred Mohr

My wife, Barbel Mohr, died shortly before finishing work on this book. Everyone who came to know her more closely knows what a wonderful person we have lost in her. Her creativity and thirst for knowledge were immeasurable, including Indian gurus, spiritual ways of bringing up children, alternative methods of healing, Hawaiian Ho'oponopono, the world financial crisis, metaphysics. No one could absorb a subject quite like Barbel, be inspired by it and then recount it in her very own voice – without beating about the bush. She did it in a way that made even complicated subjects very easy to understand. She was a wonderful networker, continuously gathering information and sharing it with the whole world. Her natural aura fascinated many people in her lectures and she leaves a legacy of more than 25 books, which have been translated into over 21 languages. I will continue her spiritual work as best I can. However I would like to end here with the epilogue that she herself wrote for this book.

♥ ♥ ♥ ♥

Even if you are a professor, a Nobel Prize winner, an academic, allow yourself to enjoy the simple things in life more often. Love for yourself and the glow of inner happiness it brings are very simple things and we often only have to allow the simple things to return to our lives. At the same time, we have to set boundaries for our rational mind when it provides us with 'reasons to act against the happiness of loving yourself'. This is often harder, the more rational understanding one possesses. It is wonderful to have it, but when it comes to love, the rational mind should accept that it can be put on pause. Allow yourself to pass through the world with an open heart!

Resources

Hay House titles by Barbel and Manfred Mohr

Books

The 21 Golden Rules for Cosmic Ordering (2011)

Cosmic Ordering for Beginners (2010)

Cosmic Ordering: The Next Step (2009)

Instant Cosmic Ordering: Using Your Emotions To Get the Life You Want, Now! (2008)

DVD

Cosmic Ordering: Why It Works (2009)

Cards

Cosmic Ordering Oracle Cards (2007)

Addresses and Links

Barbel Mohr: www.baerbelmohr.de

Manfred Mohr: www.manfredmohr.de

Ramona the healer: www.rastoa.de

Notes

Notes

Notes

Notes

Join the **HAY HOUSE** *Family*

As the leading self-help, mind, body and spirit publisher in the UK, we'd like to welcome you to our community so that you can keep updated with the latest news, including new releases, exclusive offers, author events and more.

Sign up at www.hayhouse.co.uk/register

Like us on Facebook at Hay House UK

Follow us on Twitter @HayHouseUK

www.hayhouse.co.uk

Hay House Publishers
Astley House, 33 Notting Hill Gate, London W11 3JQ
020 3675 2450 info@hayhouse.co.uk

ABOUT THE AUTHOR

Barbel Mohr was a photojournalist, photo editor and graphic designer, before she picked up writing as a hobby in 1995. Her first book *Cosmic Ordering* was initially sold only in photocopied form, until publishers Omega turned it into a real book. Many books were to follow: 'wish' books, children's books, relationship guides and books on the subject of 'healing'. Barbel Mohr has made three films, including *Barbel Mohr's Cosmic Ordering* and *Together Not Alone*.

She has sold more than 2.5 million books so far. From 1995 she began to hold lectures and give seminars. Her twins were born in 2001. Barbel Mohr died at the end of October 2010, shortly before work was completed on this book. Her husband Manfred Mohr continues her work.

Manfred Mohr has a doctoral degree in chemistry. Today, he works as an author, seminar leader and coach in the fields of astrology, numerology and on the subjects of wish-fulfilment, 'the feeling heart' and awareness. He held many seminars jointly with his wife, Barbel. He lives with their twins, close to Munich.

www.baerbelmohr.de